~^ 05.

To Albe Steiner

In memory of the master
who taught me so much
with enthusiasm and generosity;
in memory of the graphic designer
whose exacting work, sincere
and spontaneous, was always
a sound reference;
in memory of the man and friend
with whom I shared
so many ideals.

Antonio Tubaro

Antonio and Ivana Tubaro

lettering

studies and research
on the evolution of writing
and print typefaces

ISTITUTO EUROPEO DI DESIGN

IDEA BOOKS

English Translation
Stuart Ainsley Thom

Lay-out and Art Direction
Antonio and Ivana Tubaro

Printed in Italy
Conti Tipocolor S.r.l., Firenze

Collection of Istituto Europeo di Design
directed by
Aldo Colonetti
Luca Scacchetti

© Copyright 1994
for English edition
© Copyright 1992
Idea Books
via Vigevano 41
Milan – Italy

Distributed by Thames and Hudson
30 Bloomsbury Street
London WC1 B 3 QP

ISBN 88-7017-118-3

Index

Lettering as style and civic duty

In any discipline criteria exist which are the constants, without which it is not possible to give a finished sense to one's thoughts and actions other than as a series of corrupting variables and it is not easy, especially with some so-called creative activities, to restrain one's own inclinations and work inside a compositive order that belongs to all those who use it.

The humility of reason when faced with the creativity of those who have no disciplinary constraints: for this reason one must be absolutely modern, particularly in one's choice of language so that one may be understood by anyone in society or else risk contributing to a cacophony of signs and things, an almost primeval state which preceeds the definition of social order. For this reason, lettering is the basis of graphic design, one can say that the modern project is unthinkable without an education which places meaning inside the forms, solids and spaces of letters, so that they may be both easily read and clearly understood.

Antonio Tubaro is a great exponent of lettering; he has an historical knowledge, he always designs with regard to the importance of the typeface and above all he has an extraordinary ability to teach young designers the need to understand the rules of language before trusting their own creative instincts. He belongs to that tradition of graphic design which since the second world war, in a country both morally and physically completely reconstructed has honoured its typographic and compositive culture to produce texts and writings to give the young a sense of history and civic duty.

For Tubaro, to teach lettering has never meant to teach form, to concentrate only on appearance while leaving the content to others. He cannot separate the form of a letter from its history and its cultural relationships because the material conditions of language are an intrinsic part of every typeface and word and in an epoch where all expression is levelled out as if the world were not the result of cultural, political and ideological differences, it is important to remember that language is not a 'self-service' from which one may freely choose. This was the essence of the extraordinary design experience that was the famous Scuola del Libro of the Società Umanitaria at Milan, where some of the most important graphic designers of recent decades were trained.

It was an extraordinary building in the city centre where modern architecture gave way to a series of 16th century cloisters. One breathed history in the spaces and the craft of graphic design was present in the odours of printing inks and in the workshops: culture was not an abstract condition. Albe Steiner was the director, promoter and inventor of this, an inventor in the sense that by reviving the great 19th century tradition of the school of arts and crafts and by calling around him graphic designers, intellectuals and the young, he created a place where one breathed theory and practice and learnt that the spread of writing was an important way to liberate men from ignorance and create a more just society.

Antonio Tubaro breathed this air, teaching graphics and lettering for many years at the Scuola del Libro. This book dedicated to lettering is in part the result of this long teaching experience, subsequently carried out at the Department of Graphic Design of the Istituto Europeo di Design in Milan, his teaching always interwoven with his professional work.

This too is an extraordinary quality, very rare in the great professionals; to be able to teach without forgetting the basic laws of such ancient disciplines as language and communication. Reading this book, its clear intention is to always relate the form of a letter to its historical, cultural and artistic contexts, even when describing realities far away in time. Lettering is an anchor of safety, I believe, in a world where the logic of indifference is ever more dominant, as if everything was equal. People, their cultures and their material conditions are and will always be irreducible to a single universal model and lettering, essentially, teaches that to acknowledge these differences is fundamental to speaking to and above all understanding others.

Language is not only form: it is also content, the result of conflicts, drama and violence but the only place that we have in which to work, think and live and where it also possible to create the new. Antonio Tubaro's book recognises this and something else as well: that to communicate means first of all to know the right material conditions in which to recognise other languages and histories. Tolerance develops only through the knowledge of other cultures: to know the constructive mechanisms of lettering is to allow us to make our messages universal without forgetting our own origins and identity.

This is the true meaning of Tubaro's book; that writing should be understood as a series of rules for design and above all as a place for the development of culture in which people can emancipate themselves in their respect for the expressions of others.

Aldo Colonetti

Authors' note

This book is the fruit of long teaching experience in the field of lettering; its origins are in the 1970s with the lessons held at the 'Scuola del Libro' at the Società Umanitaria at Milan and continued today (thanks to the teaching) at the Dipartimento di Grafica Superiore of the Istituto Europeo di Design in Milan.

The writing of this text and the organisation of the show on Lettering that took place at Ravenna in May 1992 at the Museo dell'Arredo Contemporaneo, were a unique opportunity to order and finally make use of, on behalf of one hopes, a wide audience a good part of the rich and extensive materials collected in many years of painstaking archive work.

The purpose of this is to create a tool for the knowledge and investigation of design, useful for students and professionals alike.
The book, in the form of a manual, comprises images and tables of references but above all, exercises and projects born thanks to an intense and impassioned collaboration between teachers and students; the text, in a conciously clear and instructive style, represents in an amplified form the notes made in theoretical support of the lessons.

The word 'lettering' means that which studies the morphology of letters, particularly typefaces, while supplying the information needed to understand them and the elements required for the accurate reproduction of their various forms. There subjects, which are the fundamental aspects of lettering have been for many years dealt with by us more profoundly in courses where one gives ample space to the treatment of project themes while studying the important role which letters play in visual communication.
Italian graphic design has roots in a tradition of good lettering, which has been re-evaluated as a discipline; it is thought of as the 'abc' of graphic design because letters, for their qualities, have in themselves all the elements that can be used as a means of mass communication and the visualisation of ideas by a civilisation.

For us, there is another ancient tradition which Italian schools of graphic design have for a long time lost by not transmitting to students the common techniques of calligraphy, judging them arcaic and outdated by the computer. For a more profound understanding and so more original design we think that the recovery of such techniques and the study of antique scripts (such as 'Roman Rustic', 'Uncial' and 'Chancery') is of fundamental importance to better understand their forms and appreciate the harmony of their design.
As Diringer, the famous scholar of antique scripts says: 'to know what our ancestors have done' is 'to be able to measure the capacity of our intelligence and to have source of new ideas'.

The text is divided into three sections which correspond to those which are considered the three principals phases of learning:

■ KNOWING
At first it is important to acquire knowledge of the many forms which writing and typefaces have assumed in the various historical periods.

■ PRACTISING
The in-depth study of the structural elements of the alphabet and the optical laws which govern the design of letters and their composition which is essential for the drawing of typefaces.

■ DESIGNING
Starting with the familiar form and thanks to a technique acquired with patience, one can deal with themes of design and research for the study of new typefaces, suitable for more profound and more durable communication.

Finally, we want to express our thanks: to our friend Raffaello Biagetti, whose great generosity has made possible the exhibition of Lettering in the space kindly made available by him in the Museo dell'Arredo Contemporaneo, Ravenna.
Our gratitude also extends to the students of the courses that we have held; they showed with enthusiasm a committment that was fundamental for the realisation of this book, in particular we acknowledge the student authors of the work published here:
A. Agnorelli, E. Angrisani, C. Badini, B. Ballabio, D. Bartoli, L. Bastarreche, M. Bianchi, R. Bortolussi, S. Bussi, A. Capellato, C. Ciccolallo, S. Colombo, F. Da Conversano, B. De Tomasi, R. Dolci, S. Farina, F. Fazzi, N. Ferraresi, L. Frigerio, S. Galli, D. Gerosa, A. Giavoni, J. Hjelte, D. Jancovich, A. Legrottaglie, S. Maestri, L. Malin, F. Marangon, S. Marchioni, F. Masnaghetti, L. Mombelli, S. Morgan, L. Moroni, P. Pascolo, F. Plazzotta, L. Privitera, A. Provasi, J. Proz, M. Quarantotto, I. Querejeta, C. Seccia, I. Sclausero.

The authors

1

knowing

But above all the wonderful
inventions whose eminent mind
was it who imagined finding a way
to communicate his most recondite
thoughts to any other person even
though distant for the greatest
interval of time and space?
To speak with those who have not
yet been born and those who will
not be born for a thousand and ten
thousand years.
With what ease?
With the various jumbles of twenty
little letters on a piece of paper?

Galileo Galilei

Techniques and supports for writing and print: legend

	technique			support	

painting   stone

engraving   papyrus and stone

incising: cuneiform writing   clay

quill pen inclined at 20°, 30° and 45°   parchment

reed pen inclined at 20°, 30° and 45°   papyrus

fine-tipped steel nib  paper: commercial printed matter

lithography: wax pencil drawing on stone   publishing

ruler and compass   copper plate

printing with moveable type   newspapers, magazines and periodicals

offset printing

photocomposition

computer   relationship between the width of the pen nib and the height of hand-written letters

The pictogram and ideogram

Graphic-pictorial art is the simplest form of writing. Stone age man (6000-4000 BC) uses images to communicate, telling his story by means of drawings which he either paints or engraves in stone and hide.

The next step in the evolution of writing is the **pictogram**: a figure or symbol that takes up the meaning of the object it represents. At first the object is faithfully reproduced, successively the signs undergo a simplification: the original form becomes stylised and geometricised.

Communication through images evolves from the pictogram to the **ideogram** which, from 3000 BC, marks the beginning of the history of writing. The ideographic system introduces enormous opportunities to represent not only concrete reality but also ideas and other abstract concepts. The single characters while reproducing the recognisable forms of objects, people and animals, at times assume the meaning of concepts associated with them. For example, the circle which symbolises the sun at other times, can also mean 'light', 'day' and 'clarity'.

The most important ideographic forms of writing are Ancient Egyptian hieroglyphs, Mayan and Aztec scripts and in our time, Chinese writing. The last, while having in the centuries evolved towards a graphic simplification, maintains even today its ideographic value.

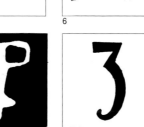
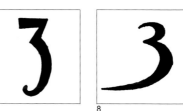
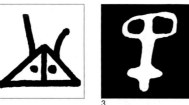
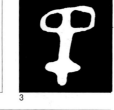

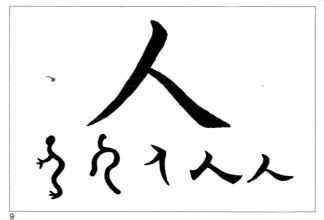

Captions

1. Neolithic bovine head.
2. Prehistoric symbol.
3. Megalithic symbol.
4. From the human figure to the abstract image: neolithic symbol.
5. Figures used for modern signeage: they are an example of pictographic writing because they replace the word with the image of the object, place or action that they represent.
6. Egyptian hieroglyph. This kind of writing is usually engraved.
7,8. Hieratic (sacred writing of priests) and demotic (the writing of the common people) version of the hieroglyph of fig. 6. These two scripts are written with a brush on rolls of papyrus.
9. Chinese ideogram meaning 'man': the modern abstract character is the result of various simplifications.
   Chinese ideographic writing is an art born of a long pictorial tradition; in few seconds the writer must dip the brush in the ink and holding it in a perfectly vertical position, trace the character on paper or silk knowing that it is impossible to make any corrections.
10. Character representing a day (Ahau) of the Mayan calendar.
11. Character representing a month (Zotz) of the Mayan calendar.

Syllabic writing and the first alphabet

In the slow walk towards the alphabet, the next step after ideograms is the syllabic kind of phonetic writing; it visualises a sound by means of a symbol, in this case the first syllable of the word corresponding to the image that the symbol represents.

With this new system for the composition of words, a kind of rebus, it is also possible to describe the abstract elements of a discourse (pronouns, adverbs, personal names, etc). The number of symbols needed is reduced, passing from a system which uses thousand of ideograms (there are 3000 Egyptian hieroglyphs) to a more simplified system which counts only a few hundred. **Cuneiform writing**, attributed to the **Sumerians** (3000 BC) and then assimilated by the Babylonians and Assyrians, is one of the most important syllabic systems. It comprises 600 symbols which at first tend to faithfully

depict the object but which subsequently assume abstract forms, due to the writing technique of incising the symbols in clay.

But it is only towards 1300 BC that, thanks to the **Phoenicians**, the first **alphabetic system** is spread, composed of 22 symbols (the vowels are missing) of simple and abstract forms and with an exclusively phonetic valence. The new characters are for the most part derived from stylised images of objects and are used not for their figurative but rather their phonetic meaning, corresponding to the sounds of the beginning of the world that is represented. For example the first letter of the alphabet is a simplified head of an ox; in Phoenician ox is 'aleph and thus the symbol indicates the sound of the letter a.

1

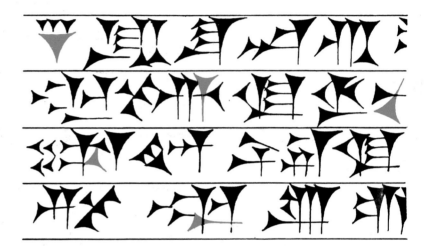

1. The *instrument and the pressure which the hand applies to write on clay tablets determine the typically 'cuneal' form of the strokes.*
   Numbers are represented by circles made by a special round and flat-pointed tool ($\bullet$ = 10, $\triangleright$ = 1).
2. *Cuneiform writing is based on five basic marks: a horizontal stroke, a vertical stroke, a simple triangular stroke and two oblique strokes, one pointing down and the other pointing up.*
3. *Ox head: the evolution from the pictogram to the Assyrian cuneiform symbol.*

2

3

H	Z	W	E	D	G	B	A'
O'	S	N	M	L	K	J	TH
W	T	X	R	Q	SC	P	

4

4. *The Phoenician alphabet with sinistrose direction of writing. The letters have a limited aesthetic value, they are made rapidly and the lines meet at an acute angle.*
5. *Phoenician inscription from Sapatba (15th century BC). There is as yet no attention paid to the general compositional appearance.*

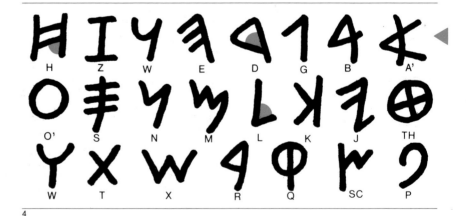

5

The first complete alphabets

The **Greeks** (900 BC) take the Phoenician alphabet adapting it to their own language. The new system, composed of consonants and vowels, reaches its final form of twenty-four letters whose collective name is derived from the first two, Alpha and Beta.
The Greeks introduce another important change, in the direction of writing which from the Phoenician sinistrose system (⇆) passes at first to bustrofedic (←) and then finally to the destrorse system (→).
This innovation constitutes the last great stage in the history of writing; in future, the transformations will involve only the structure of single letters and their formal aspects.
The canons of symmetry and harmony which characterise ancient Greece are also applied to the design of letters. The new characters, rigorously perpendicular to the line of writing, take up a more geometric and regular form, substituting right angles for the acute angles of the Phoenician letters; in some engravings, thickenings at the base of the stems also appear: these anticipate serifs.

In Italy, the **Etruscans** use the Greek alphabet on which to construct their own writing system.
The Etruscan alphabet (400 BC) contains twenty letters, sixteen consonants of Phoenician derivation and four vowels derived from Greek. Their design is very similar to that of the ancient Greek characters.

1. Inscription in archaic Greek with bustrofedic direction of writing.
2. The classical Greek alphabet: the letters have a regular and geometric appearance.

1

2

3. The Etruscan alphabet with sinistrose direction of writing. The letters still retain some strokes which meet at an acute angle.
4. The redrawing of an Etruscan inscription of the 3rd century BC: the two points indicate the separation between the words.

3

4

Roman Square capitals

The Roman alphabet, of 23 letters, adapts to the Latin language the Etruscan characters which from a formal point of view, undergo an evolution towards monumentality.

The structural rigour of the majestic Roman architecture also informs the alphabet; letter used for inscriptions and known as **Square capitals** are characterised by a geometry which is based on the simple forms of the square, circle and triangle.

The regularity of the letters is determined by constant dimensional relationships: in fact all can be inscribed on a square whose side fixes the dimension of the height and proportionally the width of the stems (the largest stem is 1/10 of the side, the minor stems equal to 1/2 or 1/3 of the largest).

The rigidity of the design is attenuated thanks to the skilled technique of stonemasons who are able to create shadows, due to the triangular section of the engraving, which modulates and softens the outline of the letters. At the extreme of the stems, with a decisive stroke, they form a harmonious termination called **serif**.

Roman Square capitals have a considered appearance which possesses all the elements whose evolution will be traced out in the centuries in the history of the letter.

1,2,3. *Reconstruction of the geometry of the first three letters of the Roman alphabet.*
   4. *Elements of Roman architecture; the basic forms which characterise the Square capitals can be recognised in the design of the triumphal arch, the plan of the temple and in the grid of the fort.*
   5. *Inscription in Square capitals; pencil drawing.*

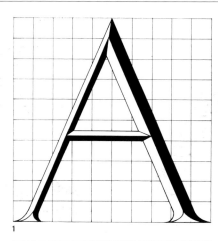

1

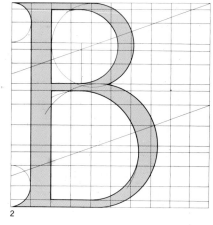

2

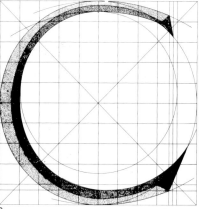

3

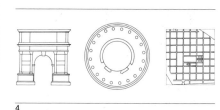

4

5

Roman scripts

The Square capitals represent the official monumental alphabet; to draft books or documents and for inscriptions of lesser importance the Romans use other kinds of writing.

The **Roman script**, made with a pen on sheets of papyrus, constitutes the calligraphic version of the Square capitals. It is an elegant writing which is used for important texts; adopted until the 10th century to produce titles of books and for the large decorated letters at the beginning of chapters.

As in the Square capitals, Roman Script has a regular height and a strong contrast between the width of the strokes; it also exhibits a characteristic serif made with single reed stroke.

The **Roman Rustic script** is instead a rapid form of writing for practical use, adopted for legislative documents between the 1st and 11th century AD.

It too is composed of only capital letters but has a less rigid layout: the strokes and serifs are inclined and modulating; the letter height is constant with the exception of some letters (B, E, F, L and P) which at times break the alignments.

This kind of writing, being very soft and flowing, permits the introduction of the first forms of embellisment: the white of the margins is at times broken by the prolungation of some letter strokes.

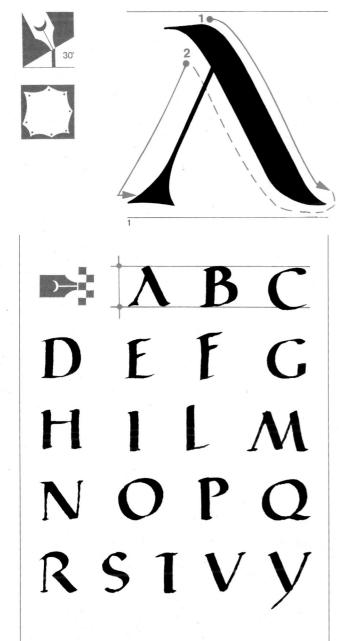

1. *Roman Script. The ductus requires a considerable time to write. The strokes of the letters are extremely regular and rigid and are traced by holding the reed pen with a reduced angle with respect to the line of writing.*
2. *Roman Rustic script. It has a quick ductus. The angle of the reed varies and the writing movement is freer. For this reason, the strokes which compose the letters are softer: diagonal lines are curved, vertical lines are wider at the base and the arches are inclined.*
3. *Roman Script. The complete alphabet with an indication of the alignment.*
4. *Roman Rustic script. The complete alphabet with an indication of the alignment.*

Uncial scripts

Beginning in the 3rd century AD, the fall of the Roman empire also splinters its unified culture; in these conditions prevails a script with heterogenous elements which are from time to time transformed by a personalised ductus.

The Church searches for a new kind of writing for the spread of Christian thought: the demand for religious manuscripts is high but scripts such as the Roman and Roman Rustic cannot be used because they have been used too often in the past on pagan texts.

So is born a new script, quick and easily legible, called the **uncial** (the name is thought to be derived from the measure of its height: the Roman inch, or uncia).

Scribes develop the form of the Roman scripts introducing many rounded strokes and some small letters; the antique 'pagan' forms are used only as capital letters at the beginnings of texts.

The equilibrium and elegance of the uncial script favour its use in the most sacred texts and valued publications.

Parchment appears for the first time in this period as a writing support; the inconvenient rolls of papyrus are replaced by sheets of the new material which beyond its use on both sides of the sheet, also permits the easy correction of mistakes.

The sheets are folded and bound to produce the first books or **codices**.

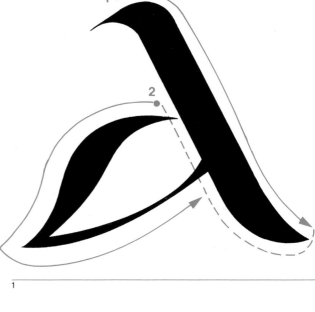

writing 'ductus'

- - - - - non-writing 'ductus'

SUNTTUTIORES
INHISENIM
PROPHETAEAUT
MANENONAUT
DEMERSIDIS
PROPERABSISTITE
TANAEANGELO ·

1. *The ductus of the letter (a).*
2. *The bilinear alignment in which are inscribed predominantly capital letters; some letters (h, k, l, p and q) break the alignment with strokes which are not yet well defined as ascender and descender. Uncials present many curved strokes, thus reducing the number of strokes needed for their production. The speed of writing increases due to the use of the new support, parchment, which presents a smoother surface that does not absorb ink and on which the quill or reed pen easily glides.*
3. *Example of uncial script.*

Half-uncial scripts

Half-uncial scripts appear almost contemporaneously with the uncial in the 4th century AD, and are a point of change in the history of calligraphy; they are born as a personal italic scripts used by scribes for their notes in the margins of manuscripts.

They introduces the **small letters** replacing the bilinear with a tetralinear alignment, one composed of four parallel lines.

The letters, reduced to half the height of uncials, exhibit a broad and legible x-height and strongly emphasised ascenders and descenders (see the letters b, d, f, l, p, q).

The ductus of the half-uncials is more fluid and simpler, favouring rapid execution. The strokes are even softer than in the uncials while the ascenders and descenders allow free movement of the hand.

As the prototype of small letters, the half-uncial introduces the first ligatures between letters: simple fusions which notably reduce the writing effort without altering the structure of the characters. Thanks to its small but practical, legible and quick nature, the semi-uncial enjoys widespread use: it is used in Europe for all the minor texts of the Church and monasteries.

The half-uncial constitutes furthermore the formal nucleus on which the various medieval scripts will be based.

1. *Example of half-uncial script.*
2. *The ductus of the letter 'a'.*
3. *The half-uncial alphabet. The letter 'n' is the only letter to keep the capital form, to avoid confusion with the 'r'.*
4. *Examples of ligatures.*

eadembrebizer
alizerquedizur

1

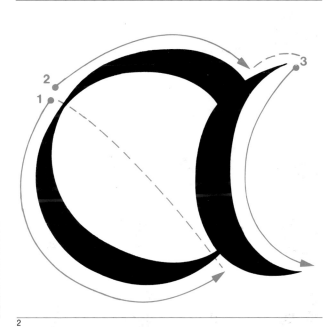

2

a b c d e f f
z h i k l m n o p
q r r t u x y z

3

4

The national scripts of the Middle Age

In Europe, between the 6th and 12th centuries, with the political disintegration caused by the barbarian invasions, a further cultural fragmentation occurs. The scripts used in this period are as many as the new centres of power; they are known under national names but change from monastery to monastery, these being the only places where writing takes place and in which this cultural tradition is kept alive.

The new scripts are commonly of a strongly calligraphic and personalised appearance and use exclusively small letters united by many ligatures.

In Italy the most widespread script in this period is that used by the monks at Montecassino, called **Beneventan** (cf. figs. 1 and 1a). The letters are very dark with few contrasts and have jagged strokes and some widenings at the terminals which anticipate the Blackletter style. They will be used until the 13th century.

The French national script, **Merovingian** (cf. figs. 2 and 2a) has very flexible formal criteria and a strongly decorative appearance which reduces its legibility. The strokes of the individual letters are accentuated, the ascenders and descenders are elongated in a disproprtionate manner and there are many ligatures.

In the Anglo-Saxon countries the **Irish** script (cf. figs. 3 and 3a) spreads; developed from the half-uncial it is clear and legible, the form of its letters is recognised from its typically triangular terminals.

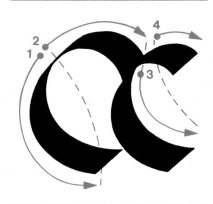

1

1a

2

Beneventan   Merovingian   Irish

2a

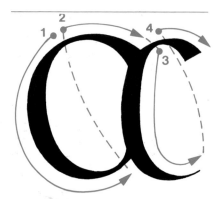

3

3a

The Carolingian minuscule script

Charlemagne with the creation of his Empire restores political and cultural unity in Europe. Latin returns as the official language and a new script, clear and legible, is adopted throughout the Empire: **Carolingian minuscule**.
The monasteries where, together with sacred texts the ancient Latin classics are also re-copied, are no longer the only cultural centres; the first schools are founded, open to all classes, in which the new script is taught and the production of manuscripts rises greatly thanks to the rebirth of arts, science and letters.
Alcuin is the true promoter of this cultural revolution; in the monastery at Tours he founds the most important university of the Empire, with a large library and one of the most active scriptoria.

The letters of the Carolingian minuscule offer few but essential ligatures (cf. fig. 3), they have contained ascenders and descenders and ample and legible small letters while occupying little space.
Some small letters (a, g, r) take up in this period their definitive form subsequently recognisable in typefaces.
Even the composition of texts is more considered: words are separated by spaces and lines well-spaced. The initial capital letters (versals) which are used as decorative elements, at times replace the ancient Roman forms with new letters characterised by their own special terminals.

1. *The ductus of the small letter 'a'.*
2. *Capital letter 'A'.*
3. *Some ligatures:*
   a. tall 'e' and 't';
   b. low 'e' and 't';
   c. 't' and 'i';
   d. 't' and 'u'.
4. *The Carolingian alphabet. The letters have an extremely simple ductus, composed of few movements. In the scriptoria research is carried out on clearer and more legible scripts by experimenting with new inks and writing instruments: beyond the reed and quill, pens with silver a lead nibs appear for the first time.*

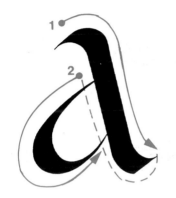

1

2

 small letter

 capital letter

3a

3b

3c

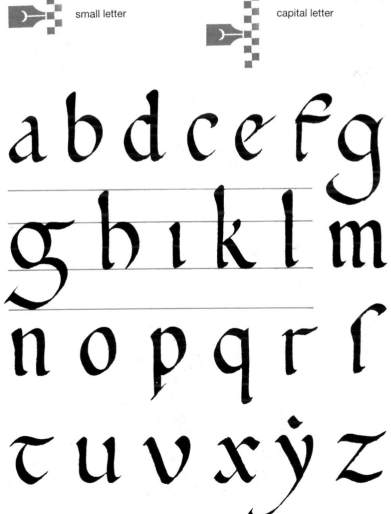

3d

4

The Textura Blackletter script

The year 1000 is a turning-point for Europe: the Crusades open the markets of the East and together with commerce widen cultural horizons. The great cathedrals are built and at the same time the first universities are founded: the new centres of lay culture.

In this period of cultural ferment, books are considered essential tools and are commonly used for study, being in demand for every kind of school.

Due to this heavy demand, scribes alter the generous forms of the Carolingian minuscule, narrowing and shortening it to make it easier to produce and occupy less space on the page; the new Blackletter script is dark, condensed and angular.

The original form, used for codices and elegant texts, is called **Textura**, after the appearance of a woven pattern that the written pages assume. It has an extremely rigorous layout: repeated vertical modules form single letters which are distinguished from each other by a few characteristic strokes. To emphasise uniformity, the distance between the vertical stems (1/5 the height) is constant and equal to the width of a stem. The angularity of the letters is increased by the typically diamond-shaped terminals of the vertical strokes. The Textura Blackletter, the common script in Germany of the 15th century, is reproduced in moveable type by **Gutenberg** who adapts it to produce the first printed book, his 42-line Bible of 1455.

1. *The ductus of the letter 'a'.*
2. *Blackletter capital letters; for the first time, scribes develop an entire alphabet of capital letters for use with the alphabet of small letters.*
3. *'Mimi numinum nivium minimi munium nimium vini muniminum imminui vivi minimum volunt.' This particular Latin text was developed by scribes as a game because the repeated use of letters of similar construction m, n, u and v) renders it almost illegible.*
4. *The Textura Blackletter alphabet.*

1'

2

small letter

capital letter

3

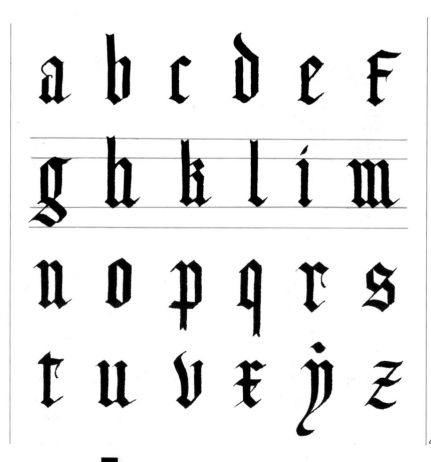

4

The evolution of Blackletter scripts

Blackletter scripts enjoy great success beause of their adaptability to the new system of printing with moveable type which from the 15th century becomes ever more widespread in Europe. They used in different countries and from time to time take up different characteristics and names.

In Germany, at the same time as Textura a more functional script is adopted which is faster and easier to produce: **Schwabacher** or **Bastard** and it will be used as a popular script until the 16th century. Its letters, following a more inclined course, break the rigid verticality of Textura and are softened with curved strokes and many embellishments.

In the 16th century, again in Germany, another Blackletter appears, called

Fraktur. The form of its letters can be thought of as a fusion of Textura and Schwabacher: the small letters have in fact strokes which are half rigorously vertical and half curved. The first expressions of the baroque influence this script whose animated appearance is owed to the numerous embellishments applied both to the capital and small letters as well as to the ascenders and descenders.

In Italy the new scripts imported fom the north encounter the ancient tradition of Roman Square capitals and uncial scripts. The strokes of the Italian Blackletter, called **Rotunda**, have curved junctures which make the letter broader and more legible. In some cases (the letters 'd' and 'o') the reference to the uncial is very evident.

1

2

small letter

capital letter

1. *Schwabacher or Bastard. Ductus of the letter 'a'.*
2. *Some letters of the Schwabacher script (first line: capital letters; second line: small letters).*
3. *Fraktur. Ductus of the letter 'a'.*
4. *Some letters of the Fraktur script.*
5. *Rotunda or Italian Blackletter. Ductus of the letter 'a'.*
6. *Some letters of the Italian Blackletter script.*

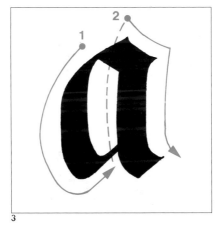

3

4

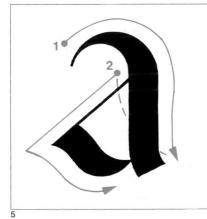

5

6

The classical letters of the Renaissance

In art, the Renaissance marks the return of the classical canons of composition. The great works of antiquity are points of reference, studied attentively for proportion and geometric rigour.

Even the Latin alphabet, in the form of the Square capitals, is the subject of analysis by artists and mathematicians in order to discover its constructional principles. The new alphabets do not find concrete typographic applications but are an important reference for letter designers who, in the design of print typefaces, are inspired by these theories.

In 1463 **Felice Feliciano** designs the **Alphabetum Romanum** whose letters are all constructed on a square, its diagonals and inscribed circle. This geometry controls the proportions of the stems, being equal to one tenth the

side of the square. The faithful representation of the classical monumental letters confers a highly decorative appearance on the Alphabetum; Feliciano in fact draws with a coloured shadow the contrast of light and dark, produced by the technique of engraving, typical of Roman Square capitals.

In 1509 **Luca Pacioli** gives to printing the tract 'De Divina Proportione'. Dedicated 'to all perspicacious and curious minds', it concerns the 'various questions of the most secret science' and the geometric construction of an alphabet called by him the **Alphabeto Dignissimo Antico**. As Feliciano, so Pacioli designs his own letters on the geometric principle of the square and circle; the proportional module which fixes the width of the stems is one ninth the side of the square.

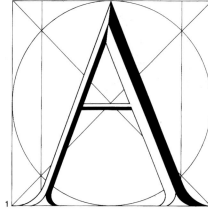

1

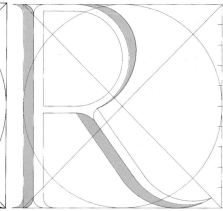

2

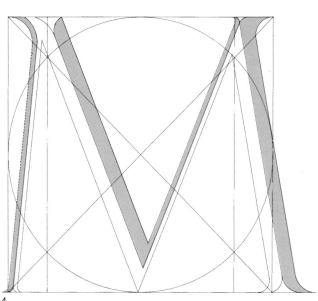

4

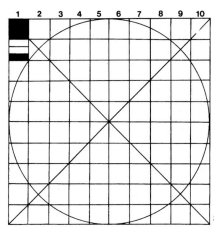

3

3. *'In ancient use, the letter is obtained by the scheme of the circle and the square and is based on the perfect number which is ten'.*

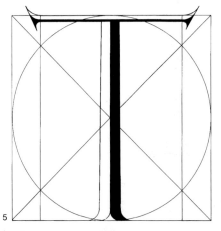

5

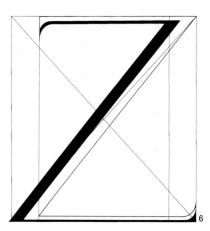

6

1. *'The largest stem may be the tenth part of the height and in this way will derive itself from the circle and from the square; and the above-mentioned letter may start where the diagonals of the square meet the circumference'.*
2. *'The above-mentioned letter follows for the most part the rule of the P; the tail of the R is traced more by practice than by reason so one must experiment more and trace it well'.*
4. *The geometric scheme of the letters is at times broken in favour of a perceptibly more harmonious form: 'I tell you that usually the letter M occupies all the lower side of the square with the addition of one tenth'.*
5. *'The letter T can be compared to the I with the exception of the upper transverse stroke which terminates at the point at which the diagonals meet the circumference'.*
6. *'Trace the line from the two opposite lettices as you see; then add to the letter with a stroke on the right and one on the left. And the lower stroke finishes on the extreme side of the square and the upper stroke should not overlap the line where the diagonals meet the circle, then the letter will be good'.*

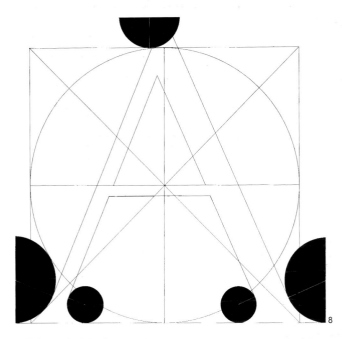

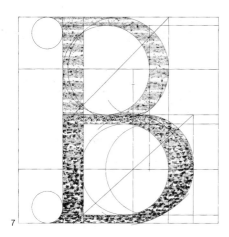

8. 'This letter A is derived from the circle and the square: the right arm must be the width of one ninth of the height [of the square]. The left arm must be half of the widest arm. The centre arm must be the third of the widest. The breadth of the letter is such that any arm passes the median line of the square and the centre arm is lower than the indicated diameters as you see'.

9. Geometric scheme adopted by Luca Pacioli for the design of the letters of his Alphabeto Dignissimo; the black areas indicate the width of the stems.

(This O is very perfect.)

Queſto.O.eperfectiſſimo.

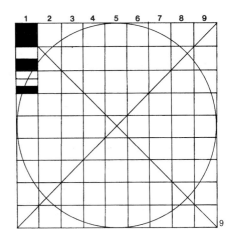

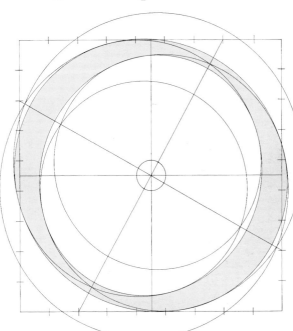

11. 'This letter E is derived from the circle and the square. The widest arm is one ninth [of the height of the square]. The upper arm is half of the widest as is the lower arm. The centre arm is one third the width of the widest as the centre arm of the A and the above-mentioned letter is as wide as a half of the square and so it will be very perfect'.

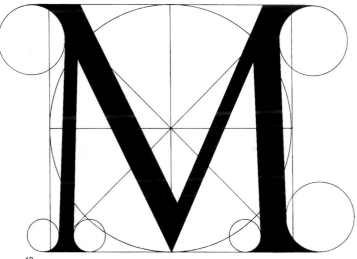

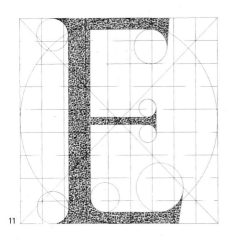

10. 'This letter M is derived from the circle and the square. The fine arms are the half of the thick arms as the left-hand arm of the A. The external arms are re-entrant with respect to the square. The centre arms are between the extremes and the points of intersection of the diameters. The dimensions of the stems are referred to the scheme of the A as you can clearly understand from the figure'.

Francesco Griffo and Claude Garamond

In 15th century Italy, gifted printers such as the Germans Pannartz and Hann and the Frenchman Jenson, open their first typographic workshops respectively at Subiaco, Rome and Venice.

The adoption of the revolutionary technique of printing with moveable type finally separates the paths along which calligraphy and typography will now develop.

Nothwithstanding this, the fascination with the handwritten book does not end, so that the first designers develop new letters for adoption in printing inspired by the Littera Antiqua, the script used by humanist writers.

At Venice in the printing workshop of **Aldo Manuzio**, works **Francesco Griffo** (1450-1518), the designer of various typefaces, amongst which a roman and an italic. The former, called **Bembo,** is first used in 1495 for the text of the famous book 'De Aetna', inspired for its upper case by Roman Square capitals and for its lower case by humanist minuscule scripts. The latter typeface **Aldino** is specially designed for the printing of a series of Latin classics and imitates the manuscripts of Petrarch. Bembo is used throughout Europe as a model by the most important letter designers of the time: Tory, Colines and Garamond.

Claude Garamond (1480-1561) designs in 1531 for the French printing house **Estienne** a roman face, complete with numerals and punctuation, where the new Venetian letters (so-called because of the subtle curvature of their terminals (cf. fig. 2), also typical of Bembo) are of improved proportion and legibility thanks to a design which minutely considers the contrasts between solids and spaces and the relationships between the widths of stems.

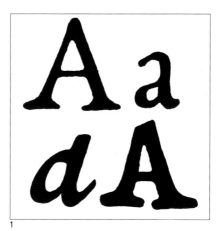
1

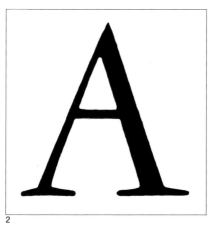
2

3

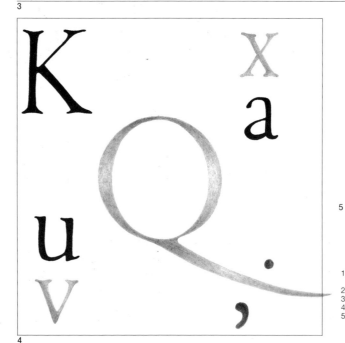

4

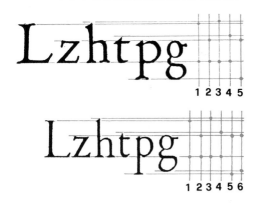

5

1. *Francesco Griffo. Bembo roman and Aldino italic. The very tight bowl of the lower case 'a' is a characteristic also used by Garamond.*
2. *Garamond. Upper-case 'A'.*
3. *Garamond. Lower-case italics.*
4. *Garamond. Composition of letters.*
5. *Alignment and scheme of the heights of Bembo and Garamond; the ascenders in both cases overlap the upper case; Garamond is characterised by very long ascenders and descenders, equal to the typeface's x-height.*

Chancery cursive

Griffo's Aldino typeface includes sixty-five kinds of ligature, for which reason it enjoys little success.

In 1522 **Ludovico degli Arrighi**, called the Vicentino (d. 1527) describes in his 'La Operina' a new italic called **Chancery cursive**, originally developed as a practical and legible script. A year later, Arrighi converts it for use as a typeface in his second important work, entitled 'Il modo de temperare le penne con le varie sorti de littere'.
This elegant cursive typeface, known outside Italy as **italic**, is used as a model, particularly in France, by many typographers.
Its letters are characterised by fine stokes of regular inclination and by long ascenders and descenders which are rounded at the terminals and folded into harmonious curves.

From the middle of the 16th century, the exclusive use of italics for text becomes increasingly rare so that today italics are mainly used to highlight some passages against the background of the printed page.

In the same years, at Venice, the calligrapher **Giovanni Antonio Tagliente** (d. 1531), publishes a new tract in which he describes various and fantastic scripts which thanks to their decorative and extravagant appearance will be especially appreciated in the Baroque period.

1. *A. Tagliente. Some decorative letters. (1524)*
2. *Chancery cursive*

A B C D E F G H
I K L M N O P Q
R S T U V X Y Z

a b c d e f g h i k l m
n o p q r s t u v x y z

2

Baroque scripts

The Baroque spirit, recognising movement and energy as fundamental properties of all things in an infinite cosmos, is set in opposition to the closed systems, perfectionism and formal rigour of the Renaissance.

The visual arts, including graphic design are influenced by the expression of these principles; the order of the Renaissance page, based on harmonious proportions and the balanced contrast of letters, is broken by superabundant decoration which fills the surfaces and suffocates text which is itself already ornate.

The development of calligraphy between the sixteenth and eighteenth centuries reaches forms of sumptuous elaboration which is favoured by the invention of **copper-plate engraving** and in writing, by the use of fine and flexibly-nibbed pens which allow free movement of the hand. The master French calligrapher, **Louis Barbedor** (1589-1670) describes in a manual published towards 1650 two kinds of script, the **Financière** and the **Bàtarde**. A century later, another professor, **Charles Paillasson**, describes in detail in a chapter of Diderot and D'Alembert 's 'Grande Encyclopédie', the formal principles and techniques of such scripts: the **Ronde** (similar to the Financière but more difficult and elaborate) and the **Bàtarde** or **Italiana** (elegant, used at court for manuscripts which are to be archived). He also describes a third script, the **Coulée** which thanks to the speed at which it can be written is adopted as the script of common use.

Coulée also appears as a typeface in **Fournier**'s catalogue of 1764. In a period of supremacy for calligraphy, the Fournier family of printers raises the fortunes of international typography; they introduce improved printing techniques and distribute new flourishes and typefaces, decorated with fashionable ornaments.

1. *Baroque initials.*
2. *Ronde. Capital letters with an indication of the proportions of the alignment.*
3. *Ronde. The small letter alphabet. The alignment on which the small letters are laid out is a third of the height of that of the capital letters*

Neoclassical French typefaces

In 1692 Louis XIV entrusts to a commission of the 'Académie Française des Sciences' the design for the Imprimerie Royale a new typeface which reworks Roman Square capitals while having a precise geometric construction.
In 1702 the new design appears, called the **Romain du Roi**.

Nicolas Jaugeon designs the new letters (Simmoneau the engraver and Grandjean the punch-cutter) starting from an 8x8 square grid, each module of this grid being further divided into 144 smaller squares. Into this woven pattern all the geometric elements necessary for the construction of all parts of the letter find a precise setting.

The research on classical forms continues in the work of the great **Didot** family of typographers and engravers.
The design of the first typeface of the **Modern family** (cf. 'The classification of typefaces') is owed to François Ambroise Didot (1730-1804). It appears in 1785 and is known by the name of its designer. Didot, who aspires to a perfect design through an ideal geometry, refines his letters bringing them to a high degree of abstraction. He accentuates the verticality of the stems and exaggerates the contrast between them, reducing the minor strokes and serifs to an essential, filiform structure.
For these characteristics, the Didot typeface lends itself to use on broad clean surfaces which emphasise the contrast between 'whites' and 'blacks'.

1,2. *Romain du Roi. Upper-case letters.*
  3. *Didot. Geometric construction of the upper case 'Q'.*
  4. *Didot. Geometric construction of the lower case 'd'.*
  5. *Some letters from the Didot typeface. The excessive contrast between stems creates problems of legibility, above all in small sizes in which the fine strokes disappear, obscuring some letters. The arrows show the critical points where the intersection of the serifs and bold stems causes a perceived alteration of the outline.*

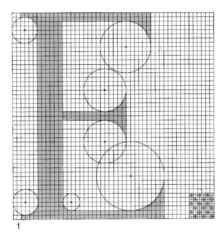

1

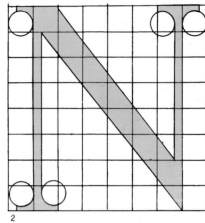

2

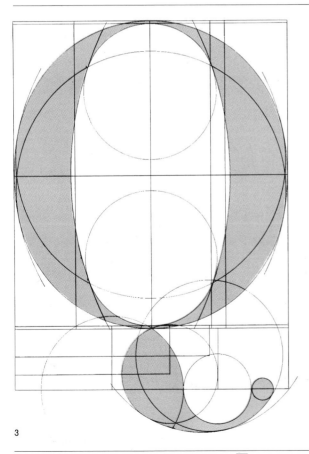

3

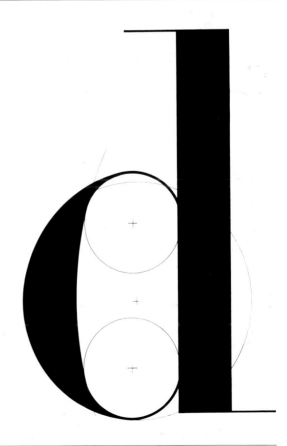

4

ABGJS abcnrsy

5

Neoclassical English typefaces

England in the 18th century lives in a period of great innovations; in the applied arts, two factors predominate: on one side the industrial revolution, which encourages the research and development of new printing techniques and on the other the new taste for a typography of classical appearance, far from the heavy decoration of the Baroque.

William Caslon (1692-1766) is an important exponent of such an approach to typography. A punch-cutter and type founder, he is inspired by the Dutch typefaces of **Elzevier**, of wide use in England in this period, as well as by the Renaissance designs of Griffo and Garamond. In 1734 his first typebook

appears: its 38 typefaces exhibit great precision which however does not exclude the use of contrivances to improve their legibility.

John Baskerville (1706-1775) is the inheritor of the Venetian typographic tradition; first a calligrapher and then a designer and engraver of letters, he works for eight years to develop a new typeface. His research inclines to the absolute proportion in the design of letters and to the highest quality in printing, placing particular emphasis on optical corrections and on the introduction of few but considered decorative elements. In his typography he experiments with different kinds of punches and he adopts special inks and smoother paper to emphasise, through quality printing, the appearance of his new typeface.

1. *Caslon and Baskerville. The conjunction of 'e' and 't' or ampersand in the roman and italic versions.*
2. *Alignment and scheme of the heights of the Caslon and Baskerville typefaces.*
3. *Caslon. A comparison between some letters in upper case roman, upper case italic (normal and ornamental script versions) and lower case italic versions.*
4. *Baskerville. A comparison between some letters in upper case roman, upper case italic and lower case italic. The softness of some strokes in the design of the letters, the open loop of the lower case roman and italic 'g' and the shape of some letters (K, N, Q, T, and Y) reveal Baskerville's calligraphic experience.*

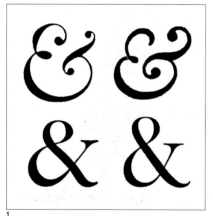

1

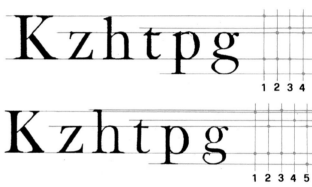

2

3

4

Giambattista Bodoni

18th century Italian typography recognises the same classical precepts as in England and France: the ideal is to pursue a clear and rigorous composition, that may be universally comprehensible because it is constructed according to 'Reason'.

In Italy, the work of **Giambattista Bodoni** (1740-1813) is of fundamental importance to typography. Appointed director of the 'Stamperia Regia' of the Duchy of Parma in 1768, he elaborates and refines the French typefaces of Fournier and Didot; he then dedicates his entire life to the realisation of a typeface constructed on regular modules with precise geometries which is also optically corrected so that it will be perfect in its proportion and contrasts and therefore functional.

After his death, at Parma in 1813, his 'Manuale Tipografico' is published, containing 373 typefaces where an important preface appears in which Bodoni expresses his theories regarding the design of letters.

He identifies the four virtues which a good typeface must posses: regularity, clarity, good taste and beauty.

He then explains the meaning of such terms: a letter is **regular** if it conforms to a scheme that defines it; it is **clear** if it has the required qualities of legibility, it is of **good taste** if it is sober and finally **beautiful** if it does not give the impression of having been designed in a hurry but by a leisured analysis and impassioned work.

Bodonian typographic compositions for their harmony and severe elegance are defined as 'monuments': the book and its pages can be considered as architecture in which each element, in this case each letter, contributes to the beauty of the whole.

1. *Alignment and scheme of heights.*
2. *Modular grid for the construction of Bodonian letters; in the upper-left hand corner are indicated the proportions of the stem widths.*
3. *Bodonian flourish.*
4,7. *Construction of some italic letters.*
5,8. *Construction of some roman letters.*
6. *Some upper case letters in the more ornamental italic version.*

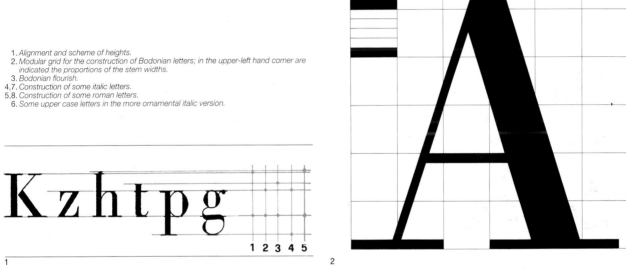

1

2

3

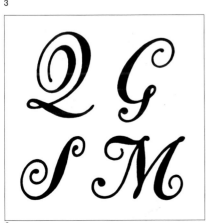

4

5

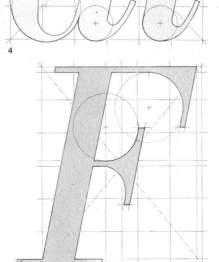

6

7

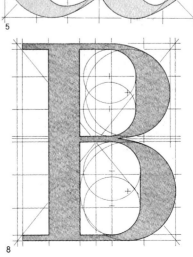

8

Nineteenth century typography

The industrial revolution profoundly affects the world of graphic design and printing: radical changes intervene to transform the methods and quality of production. The old printing workshop where an individual master experimented with new techniques and minutely controlled each of his products is replaced by a large mechanised industry which produces an anonymous product, made ever more quickly in order to respond to the growth in demand. As well as books, all other kinds of printed matter are published such as newspapers, magazines and pamphlets.

The design of letters is influenced by new romantic tendencies which prefer to the severe classical designs, new **display typefaces** adorned with ornaments and more uneven and geometrically deformed to produce perspective and three-dimensional effects.

Neoclassical typefaces are altered in tone and width to obtain very bold letters of great contrast, collectively known as **fat faces**, the most famous of which is designed by **Robert Thorne** in 1820.

In other cases, the dimension of the serifs are modified and in **Egyptian typefaces**, they assume a massive and squared appearance. In England **Vincent Figgins** offers the first Egyptian typeface in his type book of 1817. The greater part of these typefaces, because they are extremely decorative and of heavy visual impact, often appear only in the upper case.

1

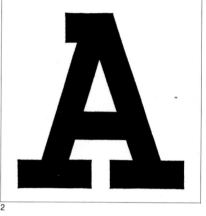
2

1. *Fat Face. Upper-case 'A'.*
2. *A French Egyptian letter.*
3. *A three-dimensional version of a letter from Figgins' Egyptian typeface.*
4,5. *'Stencil' letters, used for text on packing crates. The separated stems which distinguish these letters are cut out of a metal mask which then becomes a template with which to paint the letter.*

5

3

4

6

6,7. *Egyptian letters called 'Italian': they have serifs exaggerated out of proportion to the width of the stems.*
8,9,10. *Display typefaces*
11. *Geometric drawing of the 'B' of the Egyptian typeface Clarendon. Designed in 1845 it has harmonious forms; the serifs have rounded brackets and the width of the stems presents subtle contrasts.*

7

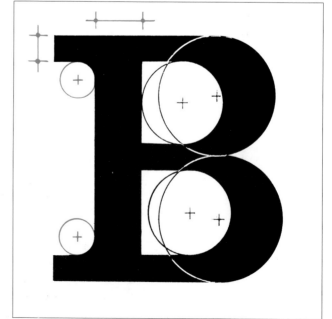
11

8

9

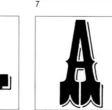
10

Copperplate

Due to the introduction of **lithography**, which allows greater freedom of design, even handwritten letters easily find applications in printing. Calligraphic typefaces are widely used in commerce or for official documents for which it is necessary to maintain the traditional appearance of the manuscript.

From England, which in the 19th century is the most economically advanced country, a new kind of script appears, called **Copperplate**. It is modelled on the elegant French calligraphy of Barbedor who had already inspired, at the start of the 18th century, the English calligrapher George Shelley. The antique

'Coulée' (cf. 'Baroque Scripts') is simplified by attenuating its strokes and embellishments, while the contrasts are emphasised by the skilful use of a fine and flexibly-nibbed pen.

The romantic taste, with its extravagant forms does not only influence the production of 18th century typefaces but also influences new scripts. It spreads the revival of historical styles, especially those of the Middle Ages. The Blackletter style reappears, laden with ornament and achieved with the ancient technique of writing with a broad-nibbed pen.

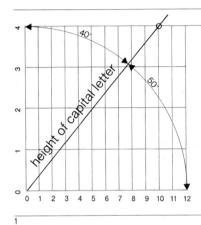
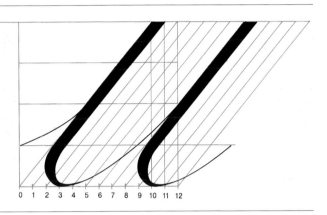

1

2

1. *Copperplate. A scheme of the proportions of the widths and of the inclination of the stems.*
2. *Copperplate. Capital letters.*
3. *The proportions of the alignment for Copperplate.*

3

Art Nouveau and Art Deco typefaces

After the excesses of the 19th century, decoration finds more interesting applications in the graphic design of the 20th century. It is no longer considered an appendage but is integrated into the structure of the letter. In opposition to the influence of the machine, nature becomes the new reference in which beauty and harmony are based on the geometry of the natural world.

The aesthetic principle regarding the design of letters for this reason abandons the rhythms of industrial production. The new alphabets are conceived as works of art, letters are expressive and justify their forms in reference to the subject or to the compositional style in which they are used.

In the style of the many typefaces of this period it is possible to recognise two tendencies: one naturalistic the other rigorously geometric. The former is well exemplified by the typeface of **Arnold Böcklin** (1827-1901) where each letter comprises a soft and continuous line generated by a point which moves along the skeleton of the letter (cf. fig. 1a).

A more marked tendency towards geometry in the Viennese Arts and Crafts is found in the typefaces of **Rudolf von Larisch** (1900), **Kolo Moser** (1902) and **Josef Hoffmann** (1905). Conforming to rigorous modules, their typefaces acquire a greater compositive efficacy but often lose clarity and legibility.

The lesson of this Viennese formal rigour, together with the themes of the new artistic avant-garde, consitute the principal theme in the graphic design of **A.J.M. Cassandre** (1901-1968). His typeface **Bifur**, designed in 1929, brings to the alphabet a strong and incisive appearance. Heavy bold geometric strokes define the salient forms of the letters, those needed for recognition, while a filling of lines dynamically reconstitutes the overall appearance of the letter.

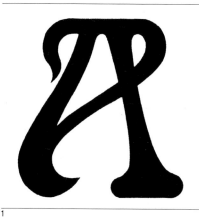

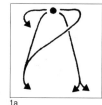
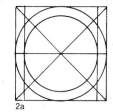

1. *Letter 'A' of Arnold Böcklin.*
   1a. *One point in movement generates the structural line of the letter of fig. 1.*
2. *Letter 'A' of Rudolf von Larisch.*
   2a. *Geometric scheme of the letter of fig. 2.*

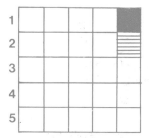

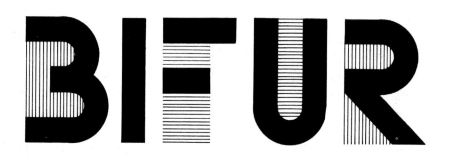

3
3. *Bifur. Constructive grid and some letters.*
4. *Some letters of the 'Theda Bara' typeface.*
5. *Some letters of the 'Broadway' typeface.*

Experimental typefaces of the Bauhaus

Akzidenz, the first Sans Serif typeface appears in Germany in 1898; it opens the way for the spread of alphabets without serifs or stems whose clearly legible form is well adapted to the new industrial reality which produces in volume simple and functional products.

At the Bauhaus School research is also undertaken to study forms which are better adapted to the new conditions. In typography and letter design solutions are sought which are completely free of decoration, constructed from a few geometric elements which are therefore easily reproduced.

Universal, designed in 1925 by **Herbert Bayer** at the Dessau Bauhaus, comprises only lower case letters based on an essential geometry: orthagonal lines, four circles with differing diameters, and three angles of inclination (cf. fig. 1). Regarding his decision to eliminate the upper case, Bayer professes to have made a careful 'cleaning-up' in the field typography, favouring speed and

economy, it not being necessary to have two different letters to represent a single sound: 'A' = 'a'.

In 1926 **Josef Albers** designs his new typeface **Stencil**. Both versions which he reduces to three the number of primary forms. In the first case he uses a square, a quadrant and a whole circle (cf. figs. 4 and 5); in the second version he replaces the rounded with a triangle (cf. figs. 6 and 7). Letters are formed simply by placing the three standardised elements on a line, thus elevating the relationship between the pure forms.

The extreme rigour of the composition is, in the case of Stencil, the high degree of abstraction, not allowing the use of optical corrections.

For this reason both typefaces, especially in small sizes, have obvious defects in legibility, and do not obtain the widespread use for which they were proposed.

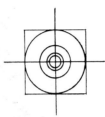
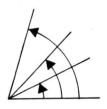

1

abcdefghi
jklmnopqr
stuvwxyz

2

add

a   b

1. *Universal. Basic geometric figures.*
2. *The regular version of Universal. The arrows indicate the critical points at which the juncture between stems of equal thickness causes black spots.*
3. *a. Universal.Second version of the letter 'a'. b.Universal. Some tonal variations.*

3

Josef Albers: 'Stencil'. Basic geometric figures and scheme of their combinations.

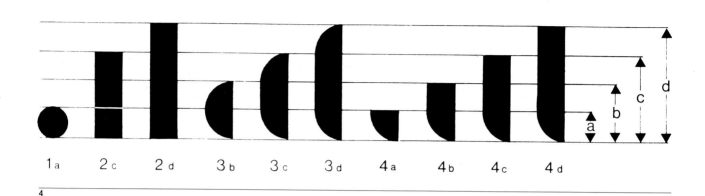

1 a   2 c   2 d   3 b   3 c   3 d   4 a   4 b   4 c   4 d

4

ABCDEFGHI
JKLMNOPQR
STUVWXYZ
abcdefghijklmn
opqrstuvwxyz
äçéšťдк123

'Stencil'. Basic geometric figures and scheme of their combinations.

6

ABCDEFGHIJKL

MNOPQRSTU

abcdefghijklmn

opqrsxrtuvw

xyzfftdkk

7

Paul Renner's Futura

The rationalist typefaces created at the Bauhaus are born of the criteria of simplicity and of strong visual impact, rules which will be observed in successive studies for the developement of new Sans Serif.

Futura, designed by **Paul Renner** in 1928 for the Bauer foundry in Frankfurt, is based on the same formal principles used by Bayer and Albers: three pure geometric shapes (square, circle and triangle) which underlie the design of the letters.
The first version of Futura shown the same defects evident in the Bauhaus typefaces: a too-rigorously geometric construction which limits the composition of letters, which above all in the lower case assume extravegant and unusual forms which are scarcely legible (cf. fig. 3).

In the final version, Renner, while maintaining a clear and simple overall form, applies a series of optical corrections to improve the perceived quality of the letters: rigour and harmony are thus so combined while following the excellent examples of the classical alphabet designers.
These rectifications are the most common (cf. 'Optical corrections') for which the horizontal strokes are rendered finer than the vertical, the junctures between straight and curved or jagged stems are narrowed (as indicated by the arrows in fig. 2) and the round and triangular letters are slightly taller than the squared letters.

1

1. *Basic geometric shapes, referred to some letters.*
2. *The complete alphabet of the definitive version (1928). In the upper case the round and triangular letters slightly overlap the alignment. The arrows indicate the places where some optical corrections have been introduced.*

ABCDEFGHIJKLMN
OPQRSTUVWXYZ&
abcdefghijklmnopqr
stuvwxyz
1234567890 ﬀﬁﬂﬄ

2

some letters in the original version

a	e	g	n	m	r
a	e	g	n	m	r

3

and in the definitive version of 1928

Stanley Morison's Times New Roman

The 3rd October 1932 is a fundamental date in the history of typography. In England, the Times newspaper is printed that day in a revolutionary format: the masthead is no longer printed in Blackletter but in a new typeface called **Times New Roman**.

It is designed by **Stanley Morison** who is inspired by the most important roman typefaces. Nothwithstanding that these years are of great popularity for Sans-Serif faces, the appearance of Times expresses an highly innovative choice; it shows itself in the will not to follow the path of formalism but in the appreciation that a typeface destined for use in a newspaper has a specific functionality which must be respected by its appearance.

Writing in 1928 for the twelfth edition of the 'Encyclopedia Britannica', in an article called 'The Fundamentals of Typography', Morison discusses the design of publications and the problems of letter design. He maintains that the laws which govern the printing of books of high circulation are based on traditions prevalent in society and therefore no typographer should consider himself an artist, dedicated to the creation of his own special typeface. Furthermore, referring to Caslon and Aldus, two faces commonly used in publications, he says that they represent the forms accepted by society and the typographer, as a man at the service of society, must adopt them either in their original form or by introducing variations.

Times New Roman, the fruit of these reflections, is a beautiful typeface because it is extremely functional: it possesses great clarity and legibility while occupying the least amount of space.

TIMES

1. *Three versions of Times: roman regular, roman bold and italic regular. Even today they represent an ideal combination used by typographers for the clear and harmonious composition of any kind of text.*
2. *Comparative table of some letters of the most important Old Style and Modern typefaces; the coloured lines highlight the different terminals and the course of the stems. The high degree of legibility of Times is due to the breadth of the x-height which appears larger in relation to other typefaces of the same size.*

Roman regular

ABCDEFGH
IJKLMNOPQR
STUVWXYZ
abcdefghijklmn
opqrstuvwxyz
12345678

Italic regular

ABCDEFGH
IJKLMNOPQR
STUVWXYZ
abcdefghijklmn
opqrstuvwxyz
123456789

Roman bold

ABCDEFGH
IJKLMNOPQR
STUVWXYZ
abcdefghijklmn
opqrstuvwxyz
123456789

ROMAN CAPITALS 113 a.C.			BASKERVILLE XVIII c.	BODONI XVIII c.		
A	A	A	A	A	A	A
E	E	E	E	E	E	E
R	R	R	R	R	R	R
T	T	T	T	T	T	T
Q	Q	Q	Q	Q	Q	Q
a	a	a	a	a	a	a
e	e	e	e	e	e	e
f	f	f	f	f	f	f
g	g	g	g	g	g	g
t	t	t	t	t	t	t

The large Sans-Serif families

Following Akzidenz, the prototype Sans Serif typeface and Futura, new Sans Serif typefaces are designed whose appearances differ in minute variations of the letters; the terminals of the stems or the particular junctures between strokes are in each case modified to confer upon the typeface greater harmony or to augment its legibility. In fig. 6 such distinctive characteristics are shown in a selection of upper and lower case letters of the most important Sans Serif designs.

In 1927 **Eric Gill** designs **Gill Sans Serif** for the Monotype Corporation: a Sans Serif whose calligraphic strokes are particularly evident in the soft tail of the 'Q', in the gentle curvature of the leg of the 'R' and in the full stroke of the cross bar of the 't' and which lead back to the ancient English tradition of the art of writing (already revisited in the work of Edward Johnston) and to the classic Old Style designs.

Almost contemporaneously in 1957, in Germany, Switzerland and France, three new Sans Serif appear. **Folio**, designed by **Konrad F. Bauer** and **Walter Baum** for the Bauer foundry; **Helvetica** by **Max Miedinger** for Haas and **Univers**, designed by **Adrian Frutiger** for Deberny & Peignot.
While Folio recalls the appearance of 19th century typeface, Helvetica starts from the formal base of Akzidenz to create new proportions between the upper and lower case and to revise some details. Its basic appearance, well-defined strokes, great adaptability to variations of tone, width and inclination (the Helvetica family counts thirty-four variants) render it an excellent instrument of communication so that it becomes the dominant typeface of the 1960s.
Univers also introduces subtle innovations, substantial from the perceptual point of view; its family, while lacking the variety of Helvetica, still includes many alphabets.

1,2. *Helvetica. The geometric construction of the lower case letters 'a', 'e', 'f', 'o' and 't'.*
3,4,5. *Helvetica. The geometric construction of the upper case letters 'G', 'S' and 'R'.*
6. *Comparative table. The coloured lines highlight the particular cuts of the terminals and the course of the stems.*

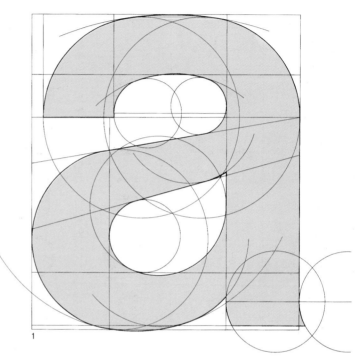

1

2

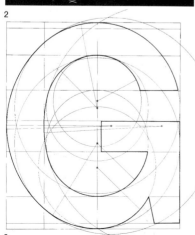

3

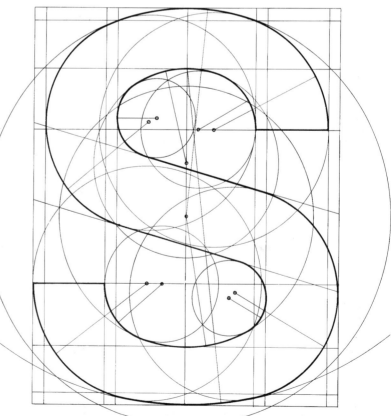

In Italy in 1965, **Aldo Novarese**, working for the Nebiolo foundry, proposes the development of a new typeface to a team of designers. Franco Grignani, Ilio Negri, Giancarlo Iliprandi, Luigi Oriani, Bruno Munari, Pino Tovaglia and Till Neuberg together analyse the existing Sans Serif designs and by developing Novarese's Designer typeface, give life to the new **Forma**. For the first time, the appearance of a typeface is not the work only of the type foundry's draughtsmen but is realised through the wider contribution of graphics professionals, the main users of this means of communication.

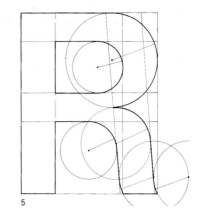

5

AKZIDENZ GROTESK 1898	FUTURA 1927	GILL 1928	FOLIO 1957	HELVETICA 1957	UNIVERS 1957	FORMA 1968
A	A	A	A	A	A	A
C	C	C	C	C	C	C
E	E	E	E	E	E	E
Q	Q	Q	Q	Q	Q	Q
R	R	R	R	R	R	RR
S	S	S	S	S	S	S
a	a	a a	a	a	a	a a
e	e	e	e	e	e	e
f	f	f	f	f	f	f
g	g	g g	g	g	g	g
p	p	p	p	p	p	p
s	s	s	s	s	s	s
t	t	t	t	t	t	t

6

Optima and Avant-Garde

'In our work we must respond to the exigencies of the machine age and more recently the electronic age […] but the golden rules and relationships through the measures of past centuries are eternally valid laws which no draughtsman of typefaces can forget.'

Herman Zapf thus expresses the philosophy of his exacting work in graphics and typeface design. His interests are not advertising, where forms are born and die according to fashion but publishing, in which the design of typefaces must yield to the eternal laws of harmony and proportion.
Between 1950 and 1958, Zapf applies himself to the study of a typeface which is today numbered among the classics: **Optima**. Its Sans Serif appearance, with subtle thickenings towards the terminals of the stems, is born following painstaking research on the 'carattere bastoncino', typical of many 15th

century Italian inscriptions. For the alignments in the new design, Zapf adopts instead the Bodonian alignment.

More recently in America, **Herb Lubalin** showing a different approach to typography, designs for the masthead of the new magazine **Avant-Garde** an eponymous Sans Serif typeface.
The overall appearance of this design recalls Renner's Futura but in fact applies different proportions between the x-height and ascenders and descenders, while displaying an even stronger geometry. Avant-Garde is a highly adaptable typeface; clear and legible, in its normal version it augments its appearance using its own ligatures and slanted versions of some letters: A, M, V, and W (cf. fig. 1).

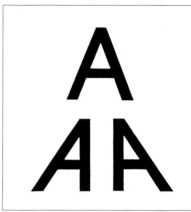

1. *Avant-Garde. Letter 'A' in normal and slanted versions.*
2. *Avant-Garde. Some upper and lower case letters. One may see the strong geometry which distinguishes the design.*
3. *Avant-Garde. Some ligatures.*
4. *A comparison of the alignments of Bodoni and Optima.*
5. *Optima. Alphabet of Optima Light and some Bold letters.*

2

3

Machen Machen

4

abcdefghijklmnopqrstuvwxyz   **Mach**
ABCDEFGHIJKLMNOPQRSTUVWXYZ

5

Digital typefaces

In recent decades, the world of typography has profoundly felt the invention of the electronic language: with the new systems, images are broken up and reconstituted in visible form on television monitors. This involves a departure from the traditional analogue form of letters whose outlines vary without interruption in relation to the technique used to create them to another, similar but digitised form which is composed of many discrete elements called **pixels**. The use of this new digital technology poses the problem of the adequate rendering of letters which to be legible must always be easily recognisable and not overly different from traditional forms.

9x5 video text, characterised by a grid of only forty-five squares, is one of the most common examples of electronic text for monitors and printers. With so low a number of consituent elements, the resolution offered is very poor and the varieties of possible form severely limited.

More modern drawing systems such as **Ikarus** and **Metafont** tend to construct letters on much finer grids (8000 lines per em quad), faithfully reproducing the classical forms. Points are selected along the outline of the letter and subsequently joined by either straight lines or spline curves. The letter is thus sampled using a generic structure on which the computer is then able to make an enormous number of variations.

1. Digital letter shown with the matrix of pixels.
2. 9x5 video text. Scheme of the alignment and the positioning of the characters inside the modular grid
3. Alphabet of 9x5 video text.
4. Different resolutions of a digitised form of the letter 'a'.
   a.   High resolution
   b,c. Medium resolution
   d,e. Low resolution
   The number of pixels available for the reconstitution of the outline determines the quality of the system.

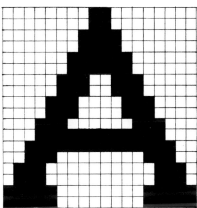
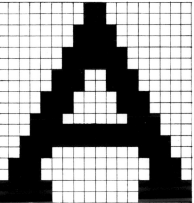

1

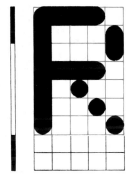  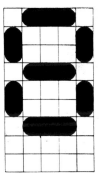

2

a

b

c

d

e

Aa Bb Cc Dd Ee Ff
Gg Hh Ii Kk Ll Mm
Nn Oo Pp Qq Rr Ss
Tt Uu Vv Xx Yy Zz

3

4

Accents and punctuation

Any discourse is characterised not only by the logical sequence of words but also by a rhythm, different for each language and by a special cadence which separates and orders the different parts of the argument. For this reason, in the written transposition of any thought one cannot only use letters but also other supplementary characters which, when united with letters or used between words, restore the rhythms of sounds and the progress of the discourse.

Accents determine the particular pronunciation of the various languages; they are the tilde, dieresis, cedilla, grave, acute and circumflex.

Punctuation marks instead put into relief the constituent elements of a sentence. They may be quantitive (full stop, colon, semi-colon and comma) or

qualitative when they indicate intonation (question and exclamation marks). Others punctuation marks such as brackets, inverted commas and the asterisk serve to differentiate particular passages of text.

1. *An ornamental composition based on the comma.*
2. *Helvetica. Punctuation marks.*
3. *Helvetica. Asterisk and accents.*
4. *Different styles of question mark, exclamation mark and brackets, placed in the following order: Sans Serif, Egyptian, Old Style, Modern, Script and Display.*
5. *Some punctuation marks, placed in the following order: Sans Serif, Egyptian, Old Style, Modern, Script and Display.*

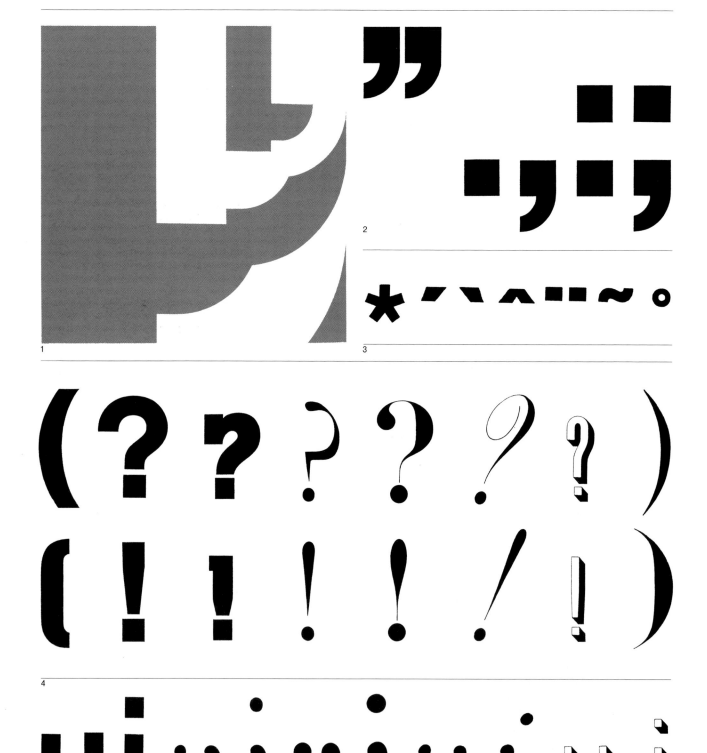

2

practising

But perhaps it is safer to limit
ourselves to say
that letters have grace
when they seem written
not with reluctance or haste
but rather with involvement
and feeling,
with happiness and love.

Giambattista Bodoni

The basic components of letters

The detailed analysis of the individual parts which compose letters constitutes the initial approach for the knowledge and recognition of their shapes to produce correct drawing and the successful design of new typefaces.

Each letter, whether upper or lower case, is composed of **stems** at the extremities of which are found **terminals** (cf. fig. 1).

The stems can be either **uniform** or **modulated** (cf. fig. 2); uniform stems are so called because they maintain a constant thickness, modulated stems are called such because their thickness varies.

The terminals, the tails and the ears that the letter may have instead assume four kinds of shape: 'drop', 'button', 'flag' and 'beak' or 'hook' (cf. figs. 3, 4, 5 and 6). The terminals have a decorative, rather than structural function.

The degree of modulation of the stems and the shapes of the terminals are the distinguishing marks of the letters and in a classification, determine the style of the typeface.

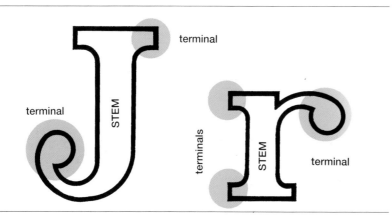

1

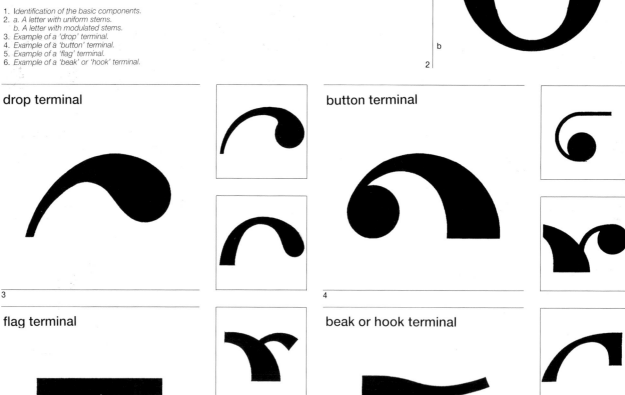

2

1. Identification of the basic components.
2. a. A letter with uniform stems.
   b. A letter with modulated stems.
3. Example of a 'drop' terminal.
4. Example of a 'button' terminal.
5. Example of a 'flag' terminal.
6. Example of a 'beak' or 'hook' terminal.

drop terminal

3

button terminal

4

flag terminal

5

beak or hook terminal

6

The structure of letters: the basic lines

From a geometric point of view the constituent elements of letters may be seen as four types of **line**: straight, broken, curved and mixed (cf. fig. 1).
Starting from the analysis of these elements, in any alphabet it is possible to recognise four distinct types of letters.
The classification of lines, applicable to any typeface, is more easily understood when applied to a Sans Serif typeface, serifs being decorative rather than structural elements.
For clarity and simplicity, while the example in fig. 2 shows the basic lines of an upper case alphabet, the classification applies equally to lower case and numerals.

1. *The four kinds of basic lines on which the construction of the letters of any alphabet is based.*
2. *The classification of basic lines of the capital letters of a Sans Serif.*
   The four kinds of letters are shown with the same drawing as the corresponding basic lines.

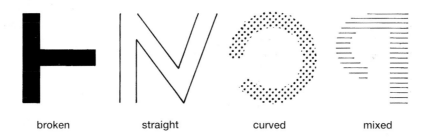

broken   straight   curved   mixed

1

2

The structure of letters: the basic surfaces

With their outlines, letters define precise surfaces; the appearance of letters is in fact born from the balanced relationship between 'whites' and 'blacks', namely by the exact definition of the form and counterform or background area.

In each alphabet **O**, **L** and **V** are the determining letters: their outline encloses the three basic surfaces on which are structured all the other letters. The three basic surfaces are respectively the **circle**, **square** and **triangle** (cf. fig. 1).

Nerdinger in his work 'Zeichen Schrift + Ornament' (cf. 'Bibliography') by applying this kind of analysis to letters of any typeface, sub-divides in general letters into three classes:

1. letters which define space with shapes having a round angle, either open or closed (cf. fig. 2);
2. letters which define space with shapes having an acute angle (cf. fig. 3);
3. letters which define space with shapes having a right angle (cf. fig. 4).

For the special cases of P, R and U which enclose mixed spaces the circular surface is considered more characteristic for the formal definition of the letter.

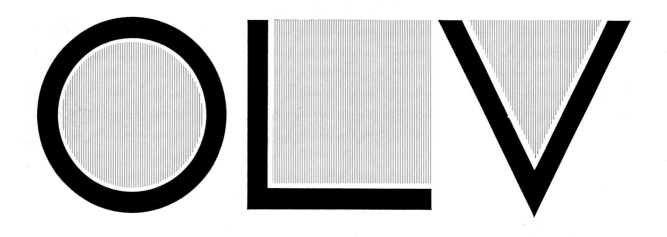

1

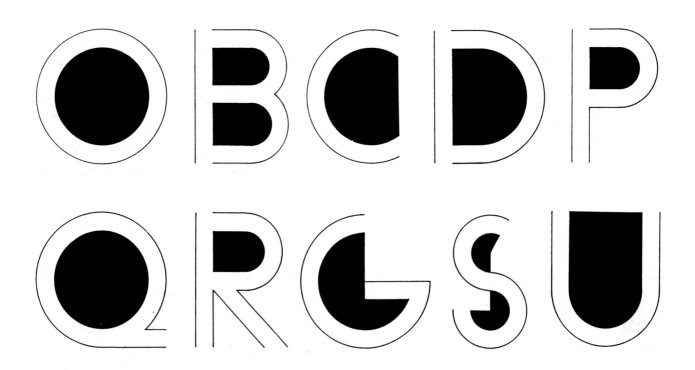

2

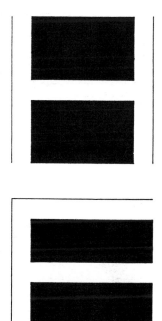

3

1. *O, L and V generally represent for each typeface the letters which enclose the three basic areas.*
2. *Schematic example of letters that define space with shapes having a round angle.*
3. *Schematic example of letters that define space with shapes having a right angle.*
4. *Schematic example of letters that define space with shapes having an acute angle.*

4

The progressive derivation of letters from the basic strokes

Christoph Weigel, the typographer of Nuremberg, in 1716 publishes a treatise entitled 'The Art of Writing'. Some observations, very interesting from the point of view of letter design are contained in the first part of the work; here Weigel deals with the morphological study of Roman Square capitals. At first he dismantles them into their basic strokes and then starting with the addition of some secondary strokes, studies the series of steps needed for the reconstruction of the alphabet (cf. fig. 1).
In his 'first observation', Weigel explains the importance of such an analysis for cognitive ends:
'This chapter teaches how Roman letters must come easily and be well learnt

and written in a good hand from youth, in a way that they result even, united and straight and not one here and there which horrifies one to see it.
Even though this method and the letter may be the simplest, they nonetheless require great diligence and assiduous care, to understand and grasp with good profit all that which serves to know and put into practice, even extemporaneously, how a letter should find its correct proportion and how the various letters may be formed from one to the other'.

(from Christoph Weigel 'Della scrittura quadrata', Bertieri, Milan 1962)

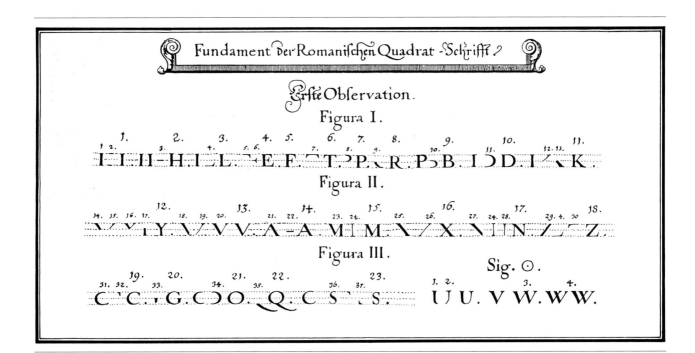

1

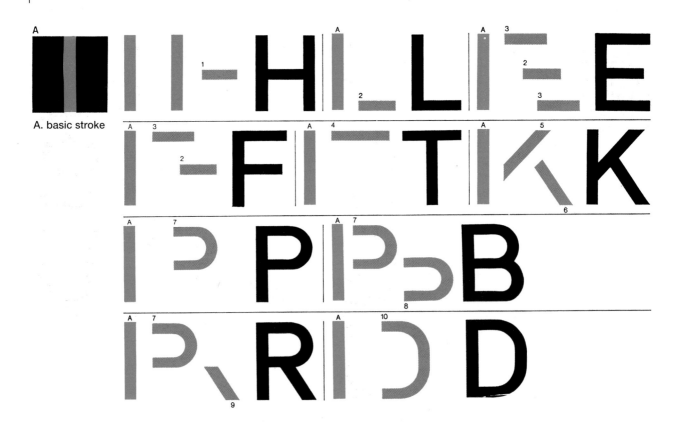

A. basic stroke

2

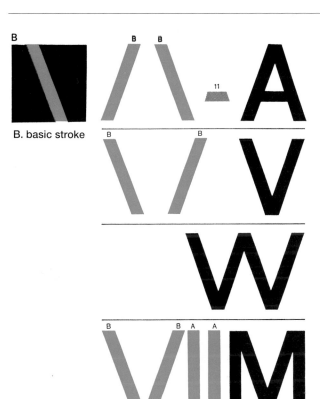

B. basic stroke

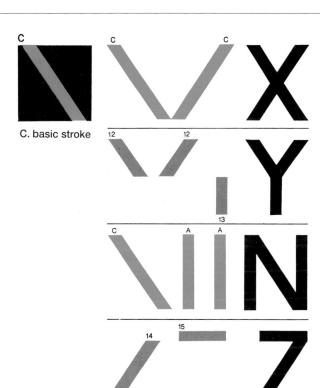

C. basic stroke

3

1. The didactic table of Christoph Weigel.
   Weigel's analytical method is applied to the study of a modern Sans Serif typeface.
2,3,4. Shown here, the four basic strokes (one vertical, two oblique at different inclinations and one round) which constitute and define four corresponding groups of letters; all the letterforms are then re-composed by also using twenty supplementary strokes necessary for completion.

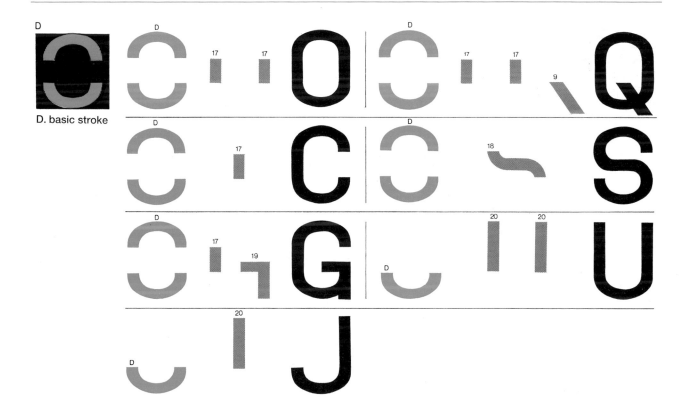

D. basic stroke

4

Optical corrections

Letters are shapes perceived by the eye and their design is subject to precise physical laws. A solely geometric construction, while rigorous, does not guarantee a harmonious and proportioned form for the letters; to obtain this it is necessary to retouch the outlines of the letters by applying subtle modifications, called **optical corrections**.
The most common of these are indicated below:

■ Letters of circular and triangular layout (C, G, O, Q, S, U, A, M, N and V) are slightly taller than those which have square layouts (E, F, H, I, L, T and Z). If they all had the same height, the former would appear smaller and would not appear to respect the upper and lower alignments (cf. fig. 3).

■ In a plane divided into two equal halves, the upper half is perceived by the eye as larger than the lower half. In order that the two halves may appear equal the middle arms and cross bars of the letters E, H, S, B and R must be aligned to the **optical centre**, placed above the median line on which the geometric centre lies (cf. figs. 1a, b).

■ At equal thickness, the eye reads horizontal strokes as wider than vertical strokes; so that these strokes appear uniform, they must be of differing widths. The same rules also apply to curved strokes (cf. figs. 1, 2).

■ In a letter, the eye reads at first the upper zone thus making it optically preponderant with regard to the lower. For this reason, some letters (B, C, E, G, K, S, X and Z) have a narrowed upper half (cf. figs. 1, 2).

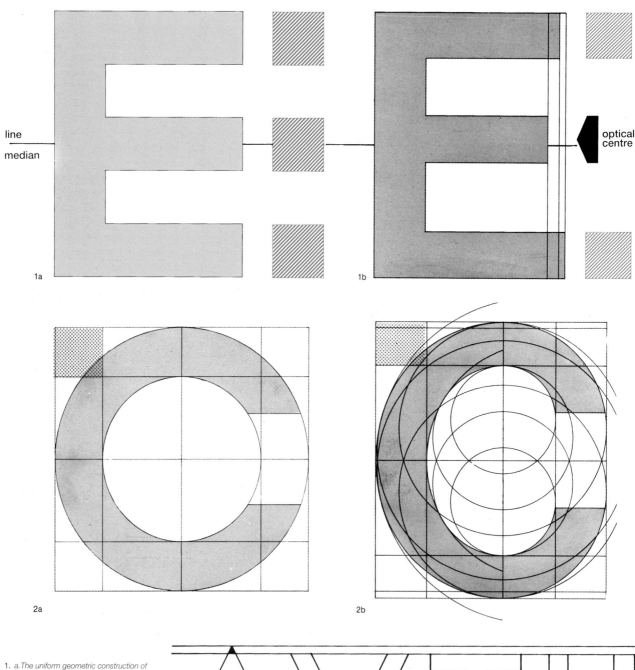

line
median
optical centre

1a
1b

2a
2b

1. a. The uniform geometric construction of the letter 'E'.
   b. The modulated and optically correct construction.
2. a. The uniform geometric construction of the letter 'C'.
   b. The modulated and optically correct construction.
3. The example shows, with exaggerated proportions, that round and triangular letters must have greater height than squared letters in order to appear similar.

3

The classification of typefaces

The great variety of typefaces makes the attempt at an exhaustive classification particularly complicated.
Many designers and typographers, even scholars of typography, have proposed in recent decades different classifications.
Various criteria have been adopted for the classification of the numerous styles of letters; in some cases the design and technique used to realise the letters is referred to (Maximilian Vox 1954), in others to the particular form of the terminals (Aldo Novarese 1956, Giuseppe Pellitteri 1963).

The **stylistic classification** of **François Thibaudeau** (1924) takes account of this latter aspect; for reason of clarity and simplicity of terms, it is commonly adopted by foundries and typographers for the sub-division of letters inside typeface books.

The classification shown in the table of fig. 1 takes the four principle families of letters described by Thibaudeau, making reference beyond the form of the serifs to include that of the stems.

The following are shown:
- the **Sans Serif** family
- the **Egyptian** family
- the **Old Style** family
- the **Modern** family.

Two sub-families are recognised, of **Scripts** and **Display typefaces** to which are added, because they are often present in typeface books, the two secondary groups of **Chancery** and **Blackletter.**

Sans Serif

Egyptian

Old Style

Modern

Scripts

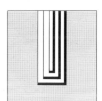
Display

FAMILY	STEMS	SERIFS	EXAMPLES
Sans Serif	of uniform thickness	do not exist	AAAAAAAAA
Egyptian	uniform or modulated	cut at a right angle, of thickness equal or greater than the stems	AAAAAAAAA
Old Style	modulated with light contrast	triangular and connected to the stems	AAAAAAAAA
Modern	with strong contrast of light and dark	filiform	AAAAAAAAA
Scripts	imitation of hand calligraphy		AAAAAAAA
Display	elaborated and decorated in various ways		AAAAAAAAAA
Chancery	for typewriters		A B C D E F G H K I J L M N O P Q R S T U V Z / a b c d e f g h k i j l m n o p q r s t u v z
Blackletter	inspired by medieval scripts (XII - XIV c.)		Aa Aa Aa Aa Aa Aa A

1

The set of a typeface

Letters are classified in families, in relation to their style. For each one of these classes it is possible to identify further groups of letters by making reference to the so-called **set** that the typeface defines: the width, tone, orthography, inclination, size and decoration.

Width

Adrian Frutiger, in his book 'Des signes et des hommes' (cf. 'Bibliography') declares the capital letter 'H' of any alphabet the example that fixes the proportion on which are based all the other letters; in lower case letters it is the letter 'n' which possesses the same relationships. The regular version of these letters tells us that if their size = x, the width must be 80% of x.
Letters can change their normal appearance by narrowing and widening; the complete series of these transformations comprises the following terms: extra-condensed, condensed, regular, extended, extra-extended (cf. fig. 1).

Tone

A regular letter has the width of its principal stems equal to 15% of the measure of its height. Letters can change their tonal value by reducing their thickness, thus becoming lighter or by widering them add to the overall black and become darker.
There are six tonal variations: extra-light, light, regular, semi-bold, bold and extra-bold (cf. fig. 2).
In the graph on p.53 all the possible variations of width and tone are shown; moving from the central point which corresponds to the regular value, the letter can take up various forms but may not support all the combinations indicated by the graph. In extreme cases, such as the combination of extra-light/extra-extended or extra-condensed/extra-bold, the letters' structure is so altered and disproportionate as to be unrecognisable and therefore illegible.

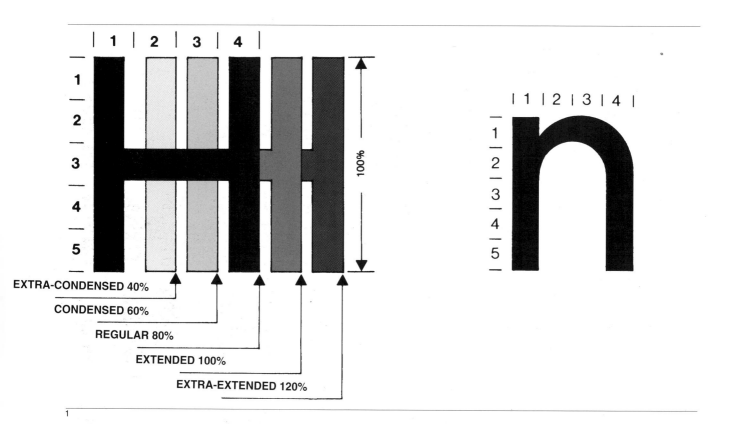

EXTRA-CONDENSED 40%
CONDENSED 60%
REGULAR 80%
EXTENDED 100%
EXTRA-EXTENDED 120%

1

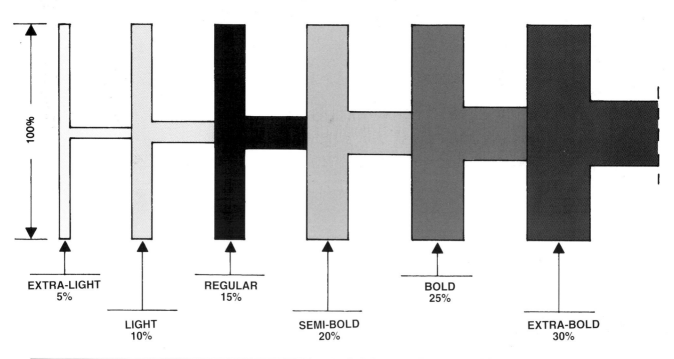

EXTRA-LIGHT 5%
LIGHT 10%
REGULAR 15%
SEMI-BOLD 20%
BOLD 25%
EXTRA-BOLD 30%

2

Orthography

Every alphabet presents two orthographic versions: upper case and lower case. The proportional relationships between these are not fixed but change notably in relation to the letter style (cf. fig. 4).

All the so-called transparent letters, those used for texts, contain the lower case and some times also **small capitals**; a special orthographic form used in publishing to emphasise some words in a text; it is an upper case equal to the x-height of the lower case.

On the other hand, there exist particular alphabets which do not contain the lower case letters; in general they are display typefaces, specially designed for advertising or for logotypes.

Inclination

Letters can be either straight or inclined, in typography the exact terms for these two aspects are **roman** and **italic**, the latter born as a simulation of handwriting.

An inclination of 12° is the best to express the italic form; inclinations less than this are not read by the eye, while greater inclinations alter the balance of the letters (cf. fig. 5).

As may be seen from the examples shown in fig. 6, the italic version does not involve a simple inclination of the letter but implies for many an alteration of form. The italic has a different 'black' to the roman version and for this reason can be used in text to emphasise either single words or complete passages.

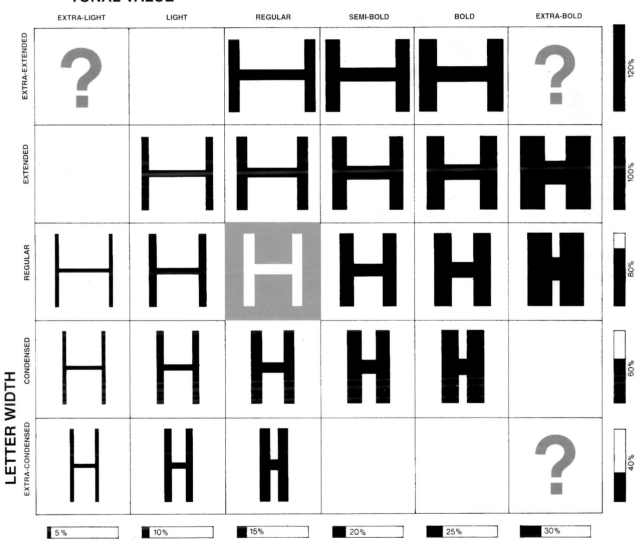

3

1. *The normal proportion and possible variations of letter width.*
2. *The series of tonal values of a letter.*
3. *Graph of possible combinations of tone and width.*

Size

The measure of size defines the height of a letter. It is calculated in **points** if referring to traditional moveable type. In this case the dimension indicated is the height of the whole type body equal to the height of letter plus the upper and lower shoulders.

In the French 'Didot' system one point is equal to 0,376mm; in Anglo-Saxon 'Picas' one point corresponds to 0,351mm.

The use of photocomposition and the computer, by giving the opportunity to vary letter size at will, have replaced points with millimeters; in such cases the dimension indicated is the size of the upper case.

The most common range of sizes is shown in fig. 7.

It is worth noting that, also with equal tone, width and size, to each typeface corresponds a very different horizontal development, depending on the breadth of the x-height which is different for each typeface (cf. fig. 8).

Decoration

With modern techniques the possibilities to vary the forms of letters for decorative ends are infinite.

In fig. 9 is shown the simplest decorative expression of a letter, the **negative** version.

It is important to emphasise that this kind of embellisment causes some perceptual problems, shown in figs. 9a and 9b.

In fig. 9a, the two numbers are the same size but the negative version appears larger; in fig. 9b one can see the reverse: equal in tone width and size the letters printed on the black background seem thinner than the positive version. To make the appearance of each equal it is therefore necessary when printing to choose different sizes of the same typeface.

Sans Serif
Helvetica

Egyptian
Clarendon

Old Style
Garamond

Modern
Bodoni

4

normal inclination

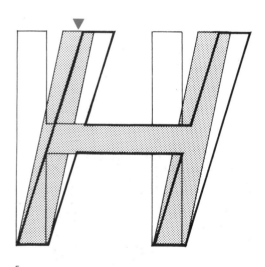

5

17°
12°

abcdefghilmnopqrstuvz jkwxy
ABCDEFGHILMNOPQRSTUVZ
abcdefghilmnopqrstuvz jkwxy
ABCDEFGHILMNOPQRSTUVZ

6a

abcdefghilmnopqrstuvz jkwxy
ABCDEFGHILMNOPQRSTU
abcdefghilmnopqrstuvz jkwxy
ABCDEFGHILMNOPQRSTUV

6b

abcdefghilmnopqrstuvz jkwxy
ABCDEFGHILMNOPQRSTUVZ
abcdefghilmnopqrstuvz jkwxy
ABCDEFGHILMNOPQRSTUVZ

6c

abcdefghilmnopqrstuvz jkwxy
ABCDEFGHILMNOPQRSTUVZ
abcdefghilmnopqrstuvz jkwxy
ABCDEFGHILMNOPQRSTUVZ

6d

4. *Orthographic variation of the main classes of characters: the proportional relationship between upper and lower case changes for each class.*
5. *The degrees of inclination for italics.*
6. *Roman and italic versions of the principal families.*
   a. Sans Serif (Helvetica)
   b. Egyptiän(Clarendon)
   c. Old Style (Garamond)
   d'. Modern (Bodoni)
   The highlighted letters are those which in the italic version changes noticeably the appearance of the roman version.

7. *A range of the most commonly used typographic sizes. The black line shows the corresponding height of the type body.*
8. *The typefaces Helvetica, Clarendon, Garamond and Bodoni while all set in the same 34 pt height and in the same version occupy different extensions.*
9. *Positive and negative of the same image, from which arise the following perceptual problems:*
   a. the number in negative appears larger;
   b. the text in negative seems composed of smaller and thinner letters.

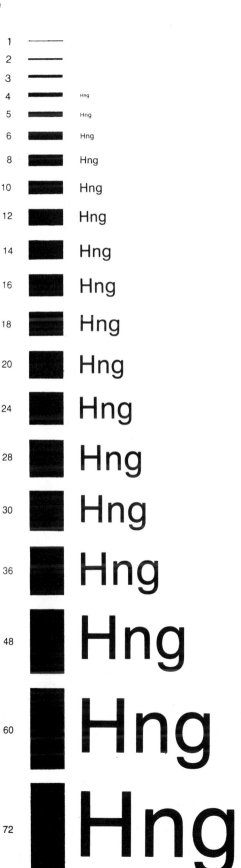

size

abcdefghil
ABCDEFGHI
abcdefghil
ABCDEFGHI
abcdefghil
ABCDEFGHI
abcdefghil
ABCDEFGHI

8

9a

Stück weit vorausfährt, damit man ersten hinauffahren, er wurde angek hat ein schwarzweisses Tricot, das für trägt eine Brille, er wird die Etappe

Stück weit vorausfährt, damit man ersten hinauffahren, er wurde angek hat ein schwarzweisses Tricot, das für trägt eine Brille, er wird die Etappe

7

9b

Alignment and letter spacing

Alignment concerns a group of horizontal lines which is essential to determine the heights of the letters. Each typeface has its own particular alignment which fixes the relationships between upper and lower case, between the x-height and the ascenders and descenders (cf. fig. 1).

In the case of Sans Serif, Egyptian and Modern the alignment is generally composed of four spaces; five spaces in the case of Old Style, the ascenders of which rise above the cap line.

Fig. 1 shows a useful schematisation for drawing letters.

It presents three spaces: one above and one below, both of a height equal to half that of the central space. Upper-case and numerals are drawn inside the first two spaces, making reference to a bilinear system; lower case letters use instead the whole alignment (tetralinear system) by occupying the three principal spaces.

Placed on the baseline, one after the other, letters make up words.

A word is well spaced if the eye recognises harmony and balance between the form of the letters and the surfaces around them, between the 'blacks' and 'whites'. The result of this balance is a 'uniform grey', an uninterrupted sequence along which the eye moves undisturbed.

The determination of the spaces between the letters does not follow fixed rules: it is not possible to establish a precise and constant distance which separates each letter in a word. The distance between the letters has to be assessed each time, considering the different surfaces that are created by the positioning of the different letter outlines.

Generally, narrow letters take narrow spacings, while with wide letters the spacing is broader (cf. fig. 4). The greatest possible distance is that between two vertical strokes which face each other inside a word (cf. fig. 5).

1

2

3

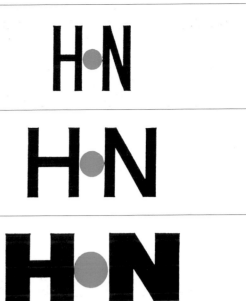

4

3. *In words, the correct distance between letters is obtained when the spaces delimited by the various stems are homogeneous; it is as if the same quantity of liquid (white space) was poured into containers of different shapes (surfaces between the stems of the letters).*

4. *Spacing between letters depends on the width and tone of the typeface.*

5. *a. A sequence of stems with different inclinations and placed at the same distance, creates a dishomogeneous group.*
   b. A sequence of stems with different inclinations and spaced at unequal intervals creates an homogeneous group.
   c. In the spacing of letters which compose a word, the greatest possible distance is that between two adjacent vertical stems.

1. *Scheme of the alignment and the positioning of letters.*
2. *The alignment of the Sans Serif 'Forma'.*

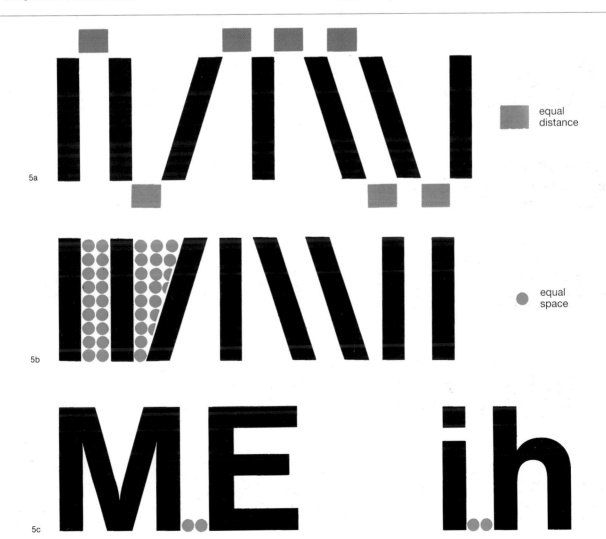

5a

■ equal distance

5b

● equal space

5c

Optical interruptions

A further analysis of the design of letters is needed to better judge the white spaces which are created in a word. The form of the letters determines the **open letters** (F, L and T) whose internal surface is based directly on the external, and **closed letters** (C, D, G, O and Q), which enclose surfaces.
To correctly space 'open' letters, a smaller interval is therefore sufficient than that needed for 'closed' letters.
Furthermore, there exist some letters which finding themselves placed together in a word, define white spaces of notable dimensions which cannot be further reduced (cf. figs. 2 and 3); such cases can disturb the compositive balance of the word by creating optical interruptions between letters. To avoid this, the composition of the word must be calibrated on the basis of the surfaces determined by the stems at the critical juncture (cf. figs. 1a and 1b).

optical interruption

▼

ELASTICO

1a

ELASTICO

1b

2

3

1.a. *Incorrect spacing: the white space between the letters 'L' and 'A', which cannot be further reduced, breaks the continuity of the word.*
  b. *Correct spacing of the same word: the surface between the letters are based on the widest space which is created between 'L' and 'A'. Reading proceeds without interruptions.*
2,3. *Examples of some critical letter combinations; if present in a word they should be considered as references to determine the letter spacing of the whole word.*

The criteria of legibility

Legibility is one of the primary functions to pursue in the design of typefaces. However, not all are designed with the aim of being easily read; in some cases, to produce greater visual impact, it is more important that the alphabet should have particular decorative characteristics, even at the cost of its legibility. Typefaces designed specifically for text are said to be **transparent**, they are in fact only a medium between reader and the text and pass unobserved. Inside this large family of typefaces is it however still possible to distinguish between greater and lesser legibility by referring to some specific criteria.

■ The characteristic zone of a letter is its upper half. Alphabets with more accentuated ascenders and a more articulate form are more legible (cf. figs. 1 and 2).

■ The eye more easily recognises common forms; the more legible typefaces present serifs which do not disturb the basic form of the letter (cf. fig. 3)

and ascenders and descenders which are well-defined with respect to the x-height (cf. fig. 6).

■ Highly contrasted letters with fine junctures have a low degree of legibility; in the typefaces Bodoni, Didot or Fat Face, the eye sees only the vertical strokes (cf. fig. 4).

■ In a typeface the outline of some single letters can be determined by the need for legibility; letters which are more articulated are more easily recognised than those with simple profiles (cf. fig. 5).

■ The eye perceives the outline of words and remembers it more easily if it has an irregular form; for this reason the lower case is more suitable for the composition of texts (cf. fig. 7).

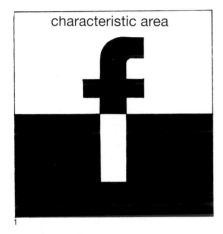

characteristic area

1

2

1,2. *The upper part of a letter is its characteristic area. The eye can recognise a word by reading only the upper half; serif typefaces have a more characterised upper half and are thus more easily read.*
3. *Terminals which are out of proprtion with respect to the structure of the letter make the recognition of the letter difficult.*
4. *In letters of exaggerated contrasts, the eye recognises only the vertical black strokes.*

5. *Letters which are more articulated are more easily recognisable than those with a simplified outline.*
6. *Ascenders and descenders which are well proportioned with regard to the x-height facilitate both the recognition of the letter and the reading of the word.*
7. *Composition in lower case has an outline more articulated than that of upper case, so aiding the eye during the process of reading.*

3

4

5   Bodoni   Forma   Helvetica

Helvetica   Antique Olive   Futura   Avant-Garde

Bodoni   Caslon   Modern   Times   6

TYPOGRAPHY Typography

The character of typefaces

The particular outlines of typefaces, independently of their degree of legibility, arouse different reactions in the reader. A typeface can please or otherwise in relation to its form and the atmosphere which it creates on the page: equal in size, line length and leading, different typefaces lend us different impressions of the same text. For a graphic designer it is therefore very important, in order to produce the correct interpretation of a work, to choose the right typeface. Bruno Munari, in the introduction to the book of Hermann Zapf 'Dalla calligrafia alla fotocomposizione', affirms that an optimal form for every kind of message exists and suggests a very simple but extremely meaningful exercise to verify the relationship between form and content.
He says: 'Let us take a known poem (perhaps the briefest): 'm'illumino d'immenso'. Let us print it in different typefaces, in Blackletter, Script, Old Style, Sans Serif extrabold. The meaning changes'.
The text shown here is the application of this exercise.

M'illumino d'immenso

Helvetica
bold
34 pt.

M'illumino d'immenso

Futura
semi bold
34 pt.

M'illumino d'immenso

Bodoni
semi-bold
34 pt.

M'illumino d'immenso

Bodoni
bold italic
34 pt.

M'illumino d'immenso

Garamond
bold italic
34 pt

M'illumino d'immenso

Landi
bold condensed
34 pt.

M'illumino d'immenso

Egizio
bold
34 pt.

M'illumino d'immenso

Copperplate
semi-bold
34 pt.

M'illumino d'immenso

Mistral
34 pt.

M illumino d immenso

Blackletter

3

designing

...freed from its linguistic role (being part of a single word), a letter can say everything... ... it can be a starting point for an 'imagerie' as vast as a cosmography.

Roland Barthes

Abstract scripts

'I do not know how to explain why it gives me such pleasure to write, almost as if a sheet of paper and a good pen might compensate me for the strain of thinking.

While I reflect my hand works autonomously: it moves, changes direction, rises and sinks, it cancels, it creates a labyrinth of lines, it dilates spaces, it plays with the margins, with those small, purely functional marks that are letters, it puts together an artistic construction.

And thus I became an artist; I do not try to reproduce reality but leave my body to express itself with the gesture of writing, with traces and marks on an intact and therefore infinitely mouldable surface'.

(from the preface by Roland Barthes to 'La Civilisation de l'écriture' by R. Druet and H. Grégoire).

Making sequences of marks without meaning, by giving free reign to imagination, helps to recover the innate pleasure of the spontaneous gestures of which Roland Barthes speaks; it accustoms the eye and hand to cooperate in the immediate realisation of harmonious marks.

It is important to experiment with new writing instruments and supports, from the most traditional to the strangest, in order to search for unusual shapes and marks.

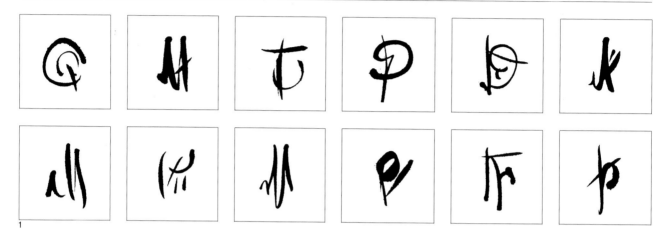

1

1,3. *Marks made on paper by a pen with a fine and flexible point. Forms often appear which remind one of letters: they are the unconcious memory which one has learnt since childhood.*
2,4. *Writing made with solder.*

5. *Coloured ink on smooth paper with an eraser.*
6. *Black ink on smooth paper applied with a toothbrush.*
7. *Black gouache applied with a spatula to smooth cardboard.*
8. *White gouache applied with a spatula to black cardboard.*

2

3

4

5

6

7

8

At the limits of legibility

Letters are signs embedded in our memory; since infancy we have learnt how to recognise their outlines and by now they are extremely familiar.

The eye, in front of a written text, does not need to meticulously check the outlines of the letters because to recognise them the reading of a few strokes is sufficient. One can thus affirm that the whole form, the particular form of the letter, passes unobserved.

From the point of view of graphic communication the problem is often posed by making transparent typefaces take up stronger connotations to produce greater visual impact; it becomes necessary to find shapes which restore an unexpected image to the letters but, at the same time, not so alter them as to make them unrecognisable. With gradual changes to the outline of the letters it is possible to reach an unusual form that modifies the initial legibility without however nullifying it.

The studies proposed in the following pages demonstrate this kind of research directed to verify the possibilities of variation in the form of a character up to the limits of its recognisability.

There are two ways to do this and in both the starting point is a letter in its positive or negative versions (cf. fig. 1a and 1b).

In the first case (cf. figs. pp. 64-5), by preserving the outline of the letter, one alters its dimension and direction inside a pre-arranged area. The succession of images, comprising a sequence of cuts, tends to focus on that part of the letter which is considered most characteristic for its identification; at the limits of the letter legibility one discovers that, not only the essential strokes, necessary for its recognition, but also the portions of space (counter-form) are involved in the reading of the complete image.

1a,1b. *Letters of reference for the exercise shown in figs. 2, 3, 4 and 5.*
2,3,4,5. *A sequence of cuts made upon the letter 'a'.*
6. *The letter of reference for the exercise shown in figs. 7 and 8.*
7. *Detail of the letter 'K' in negative.*
8. *Detail of the letter 'K' in positive.*

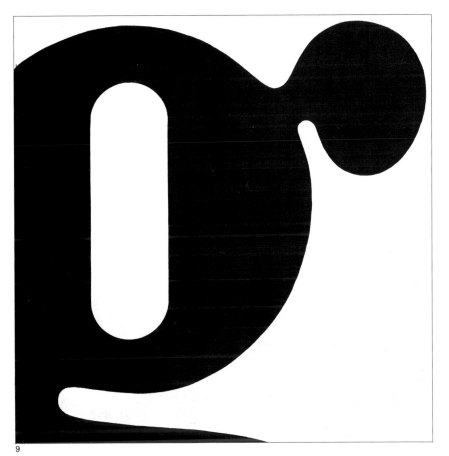

9

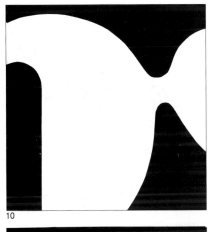

10

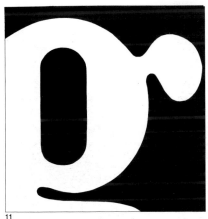

11

12

9,12. *Sequence of cuts made upon the letter 'g' in positive.*
10,11. *Sequence of cuts made upon the letter 'g' in negative.*

In the second group of exercises (cf. figs 13-17), are analysed the variations obtained by altering the usual relationship between 'whites' and 'blacks'. The examples shown offer some of the numerous possibilities for change that the letter can undergo; it assumes new characteristics by modifying either the orientation or the dimension of the internal surface; further variations can be realised by completely annulling this or by breaking up the black structural strokes and by confusing the internal and external white areas (cf. fig. 16).

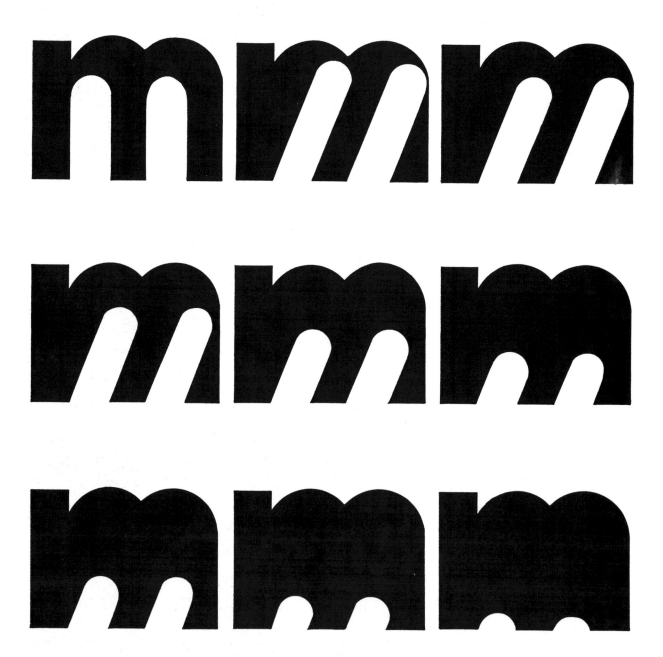

13

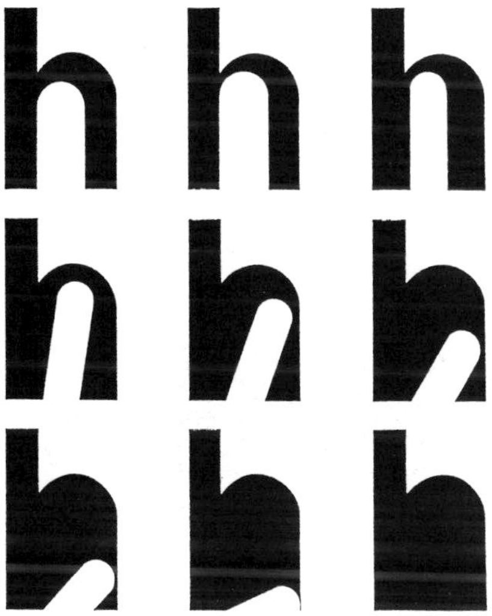

14

15

13, 14, 15, 17. Gradual variations in the relationships between
'whites' and 'blacks' in the letters 'm', 'h', 'B'
and 'C'.

16. Examples of possible variations in the shape of
letters by modifing either the counterform or
the structural strokes.

16

17

Form and counterform

'O mon âme! Le poème n'est point fait de ces lettres
que je plante comme des clous, mais du blanc qui
reste sur le papier'.

Paul Claudel

In art and graphic design, a composition is judged not only by the quality and
the form of the chosen images but also by their harmonious and balanced
relationship with the surface on which they appear.
In the case of letters it has already been shown (cf. 'The structure of letters: the
basic surfaces') that their morphology is born from the right proportion of
'black' and 'white', between ground and background.
It has also been shown that the familiarity of the letters does not depend simply
on the structural strokes but also on the spaces that they define; in this way
the recognition of a letter is also linked to the shape of its 'spaces'.
The shapes that are created in the interstices of words or between lines of text
are thus as familiar to the eye; during reading these outlines pass unnoticed
but attentively analysed can carry the form of other possible alphabets.
Between their outlines the shapes of animals and eccentric characters can
come to life, an expression of the vast 'imagerie' of which Roland Barthes
speaks when dealing with 'the spirit of the letter'.

1

2

1,2. *Positive and negative counterform of the letter 'A';
the eye also identifies as familiar shapes the spaces
contained between the strokes that comprise the
letter.*
3a,3b. *The spaces between the letters of the alphabet of
Arnold Böcklin are animated as imaginary figures.*
4a,4b. *Animals and eccentric characters populate the
spaces between the numbers of a Blackletter
alphabet.*

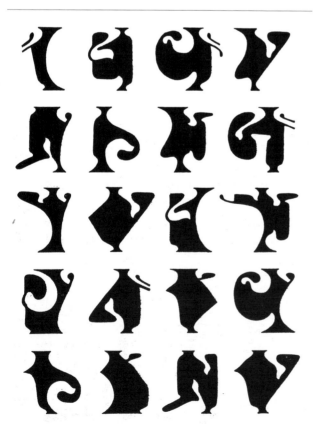

3a

3b

4a

4b

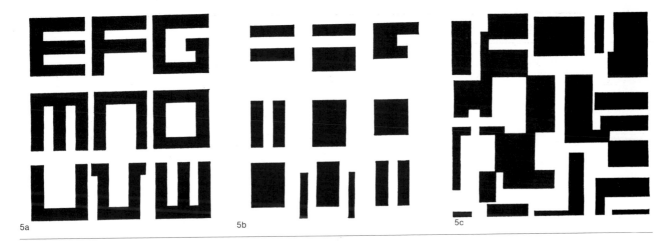

5a   5b   5c

6

5. a. *Letters from the 'De Stjil' alphabet (1917) designed by Theo Van Doesburg for the eponymous magazine.*
   b. *Counterform of the letters of fig. 5a.*
   c. *An abstract composition constructed from the blacks of the counterform of fig. 5b.*
6. *Sequences of numbers whose reading is created by the alternate recognition of the shape and background of the sign.*
7. *Legibility studies with the alternation of form and counterform in the composition of the letters.*
8. *The application of the research shown in fig. 7 to the design of the logotype of 'Museo dell'arredo contemporaneo', Ravenna.*

7   8

Ornamental typographic composition

The usual form of letters is by itself decorative; isolated or united in compositions they can accentuate their ornamental aspects by constituting modular figures to be used as special typographic embellishments.
With letters one can construct patterns, lines, frames, even complete textures in the drawing of which the familiar shapes confuse and often annul each other, loosing their formal and semantic identity. The possible combinations for the creation of new ornamental images are infinite because of the vast choice of letters from which to start. Imagination and sensitivity are the only guides for the selection of the forms to be assembled; the subsequent definition of different patterns is achieved by the movement on the surface of the basic module.

In the examples shown here the compositional rules applied exhibit the following criteria:
■ repetition and matching
■ superimposition
■ translation
■ rotation around either a point or an axis of symmetry.

1a   1b   1c

1d

1. *Example of the simplest method for the creation of typographic ornaments.*
   a. basic letters.
   b. composition of module.
   c. repetition of module over a surface.
   d. repetition of module along a line.
2. *Module composed with the rotation of the '&' around a central point. The decorative effect is accentuated by the alternation of positive and negative signs.*
3. *The fusion of two reflected 'E's comprises the module to be repeated in the composition of a texture.*

2

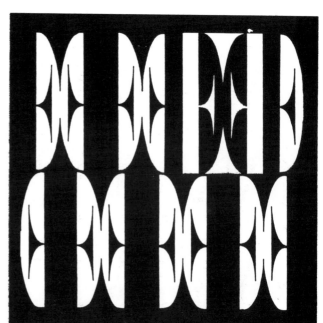

3

4

5

4. *Individual ornamental figure composed of numbers and letters.*
5. *Module achieved by rotating the '§' around a central point.*
6. *This frieze is composed by the repetition of the module formed by the reflection and inversion of a single letter.*
7. *The translation and rotation of a letter 'y' around an axis of symmetry generates the repeated motif in a composition of a very subtle pattern.*
8. *From the rotation of an 'a' around a central point is born a puntiform module; the superimposed white areas make the recognition of the original letter difficult.*

6

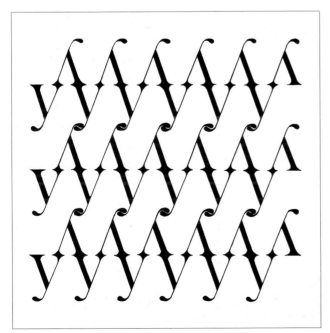

The monogram

The monogram is a sign composed of two characters (in the case of more letters, a 'seal') which have been joined in a particular manner.

Since its origin in classical Greece the monogram appears as a signature, as a symbol of property or as an identification mark on manufactures and goods (cf. fig. 2). Independently of this end the idea of uniting letters by finding special arrangements and superimpositions was developed with very original solutions in the Middle Ages; the use of calligraphic personalised scripts in fact favours the creation of ligatures between letters which are inserted in the homogeneous pattern of texts as decorative elements of the page.

The monograms of the first Christian period and successively those of the epoch of Charlemagne show in their simplicity a great compositional ability: at times ever the letters of a whole name are united to form abstract geometries (cf. fig. 6). The monogram follows the same evolution undergone by the form of letters: different styles and different applications characterise it in various historical periods.

The monogramme is not created by the casual arrangement of some letters but rather by the study of particular superimpositions and connections between them to obtain a form that may not be 'transparent'. In fact the reading of the monogram, as a strong but unfamiliar image, must at casual observation not exhaust but stimulate a process of interpretation; for this reason the letters that comprise the monogram, elaborated to augment the visual impact of the whole, do not read easily but are guessed at in the overall design.

1

1. Byzantine inscription at Ravenna; between the lines of text, compositions of two or more letters have been inserted.
2. Grecian monogram.
3. The monogram of Jesus with the Latin meaning 'In Hoc Signo'.
4. The monogram of the German painter Hans Von Aachen (1552-1616).
5. The linkage of two capital letters of Carolingian minuscule script (12th century).

2

3

4

5

7

8

6

6. The monogram of Charlemagne composed of the letters that make up his name (KAROLVS).
7. The monogram of Albrecht Dürer (1471-1528).
8. The monogram of Kolo Moser (1902).
9. A monogram composed of the letters 'A' and 'B' taken from a book of embroidery (1920).

9

10

11

12

13

14

15

10-20. *Monograms designed by the authors and some students.*
  10. *G + G.*
  11. *A + A .*
  12. *A + Z.*
  13. *M + L.*
  14. *C + E.*
  15. *U + S.*
  16. *G + B.*
  17. *A + I + T.*
  18. *J + H.*
  19. *M + L.*
  20. *C + S.*

16

17

18

19

20

By generalising it is possible to identify some fundamental characteristics that the monogram and in general any mark, or symbol, must respect:

- **clarity** of composition for easy interpretation;
- **personality** and strong character in the overall image;
- **individuality** of the sign with particular reference to the person or subject (especcially in the case of the seal).

The monogram can have various applications; to confirm its suitability for use it is necessary that the design be placed under certain checks, the principal aspects of which are indicated below:

- **dimension**: the legibility of the mark must remain unchanged whether significantly enlarged and reduced (cf. fig. 26);
- **repeatability**: the multiplication of the mark on whole surfaces can be obtained by its simple repetition or by introducing variations of the design to

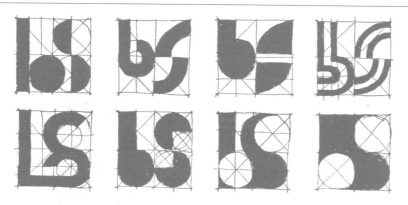

21

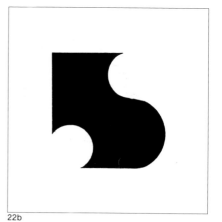

22a

22b

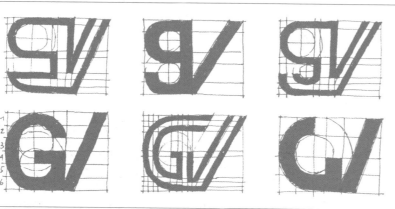

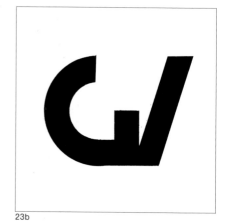

23a

23b

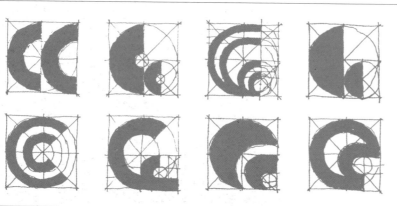

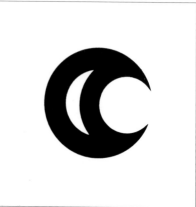

24a

24b

animate the appearance of the whole (cf. fig. 28);

■ **tone and colour**: the monogram, while not losing any recognisability, has to assume changes of tone and colour in relation to various applications (cf. figs. 25a, b and c);

■ **suitability to media**: it is always necessary to check that the form of the mark is suited to communication not only by printing but also through other techniques (casting, neon tubes, engraving etc.) or through other media (television, etc.).

21. *Preliminary studies for the research into possible links between two letters.*
22. *a. B + S: studies for the geometric performance of the monogram.*
    b. Final version.
23. *a. G + V: studies for the geometric performance of the monogram.*
    b. Final version.
24. *a. C + C: studies for the geometric performance of the monogram.*
    b. Final version.
25. *Verification of the legibility of the monogram M + S with variations of tone.*
    a. positive; b. negative; c. with line texture.
26. *Range of dimensional variations of the monogram G + P.*
27. *Monogram G + A.*
28. *Compositional study of the repetition of the monogram of fig. 27.*

25a

25b

25c

26

27

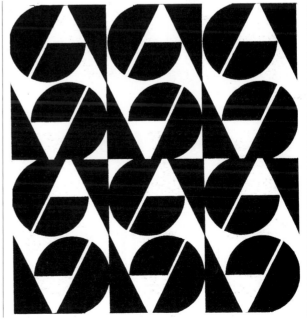

28

The missing letter

The drawing of a logotype often implies the design of a personalised image which refers to the client's manufactured output or, more generally, to the character of the subject for which the logotype is designed.

In graphic design a frequent solution is to substitute one or more letters of the logotype with the outline of an object or any other sign that more clearly defines the subject's identity. Because letters are recognised by the eye thanks to the perception of a few essential strokes (cf. 'The criteria of legibility'), their substitution by a figure that has similar structural elements does not cause grave alterations to the normal reading process. Instead, the word, thanks to the introduction of a different and more interesting image, loses its characteristic 'transparency' and assumes a greater iconic value.

If the exchange is well considered and the new outline has strength but also balance and harmony, the eye is attracted but not disturbed; during reading a process of vision and an interpretation of the image are superimposed.

In the case of the text 'Venezia' of fig. 3, thanks to the notoriety of the subject, the relationship between word and extraneous element is immediately understood.

Instead, in unknown logotypes it is actually the inserted image that by referring to a concrete object loads the composition with identity. It is of strong orientation especially in those cases where the text, being a proper name, gives no special details on the character of the subject (cf. figs. 2, 4 and 5).

1. Logotype for a packet of grissini.
2. Logotype for a new screw.
4. Logotype for an electronics company.

5. Logotype for a children' clothing company.
6. Logotype for a car dealership.
7. Logotype for a photographic agency.

The expressive letter

The alteration of the letterform can also take place in reference to a word. In this case the meaning of the word becomes the theme for the creation of a new image for the letter; the word directly affects the letters and changes them to represent the action undergone (cf. figs. 1, 2, 4, 6, 8, 9 and 10).
In some cases the same letters, without changing their original form, are given an identity and themselves become interactive subjects.
In compositions of this kind the choice of typeface is very important. Whether as an alphabet (each letter having its own personality) or as type; the 'personalities' that intervene in the action must have precise connotations well able to express in the clearest manner possible, the action to be represented (cf. figs. 3, 5 and 7).

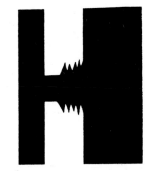

1

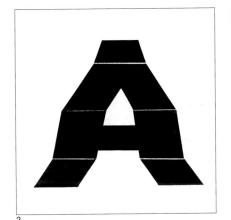

2

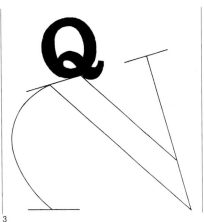

3

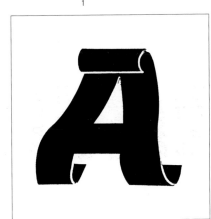

4

1. *To squeeze.*
2. *To fold.*
3. *To press.*
4. *To roll.*
5. *To pierce.*
6. *To observe.*
7. *To fill.*
8. *To multiply.*
9. *To interlace.*
10. *To indicate.*

5

6

7

8

9

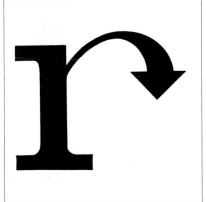

10

The typogram

It has been proved that in graphic design letters, in their usual forms, are often insufficient for strong and expressive communication (cf. 'The missing letter'). The right typeface, while well chosen with regard to the word that it composes, at times is not enough for clear expression; one makes use of a graphic solution called the **typogram** or **word-image**.

In this case the words are loaded with an iconic value dominant with respect to their usual linguistic valency; they must be read and at the same time interpreted as images: who observes them must be able to understand the contents (the figure) by reading the container (the word).

During the design of a typogram the first step after the choice of typeface is to alter the normal alignment of the letters which compose the text; the disorder thus caused is then recomposed to find a reciprocal position of the letters or a manipulated form of them which best expresses the meaning of the represented word.

1. *To squint at (sbirciare).*
2. *Shy (timido).*
3. *Compressed (compresso).*
4. *Ambiguous (ambiguo).*
5. *To push (spingere).*
6. *Perplexed (perplesso).*
7. *To trip over (inciampare).*
8. *To think (pensare).*
9. *Packaged (imballato).*
10. *Lazy (pigro).*
11. *Dictatorship (dittatura).*
12. *To strangle (strangolare).*

perplesso

INCIAMPARE

IMBALL

AGRO

DITTA URA

The calligram

It was Guillaime Apollinaire who invented the word 'calligram' by so calling the poems of a story written between 1913 and 1917. While describing his new compositions he affirmed that 'typographic devices, pushed far by audacity, have the advantage of giving birth to a visual lyricism unknown before now'. In fact, in the lyrics of Apollinaire, the letter while not losing its intrinsic sonorous quality is loaded with visual qualities as well (cf. fig. 8).

In occidental writing it is hard to reach a fusion between images and letters; this is however very recurrent in Arabic writing and in Hebrew and Chinese writing which are already composed of figurative symbols (cf. fig. 2). Occidental alphabets have on the contrary a very rigid structure blocked by a geometry that distances them from the world of play of forms. The first figurative poems in occidental culture appear during the 3rd century BC and are designed by a Greek, Simmia of Rhodes; the metre of his verse is adapted to simple figures loaded with a mythological meaning such as egg, axe and wings.

In the Latin world, Teocritus and Publius Optatianus Porphyrius are the greatest exponents of this genre; to Porphyrius (4th century AD) is owed the invention of calligrams of abstract form, constructed in particular on the square.

The components of verses adapted to geometric schemes (diamonds, squares and triangles) with numeric relationships of religious meaning are very common in the Middle Age; this type of scheme was adopted by Venantio Fortunato (6th century AD) for the creation of calligrams inspired prevalently by sacred subjects (cf. fig. 3).

With the Middle Ages the calligram exhausts its distinctly religious character. Since the Renaissance these compositions deal with more varied themes adopting, above all in the Baroque period, decorative images elaborated

1. *Disc of Festo (Crete) dating from 2000 BC. The disc is engraved with syllabic signs which represent animals, people and objects of daily use; the disc is read by starting at the edge and working towards the centre.*
2. *A composition in 'Kufi' script (a particular Arabic script of squared shape from the city of Koufa from which it derives its name) representing a mosque.*
3. *A figurative poem in the shape of a cross by Venantio Fortunato (6th century AD).*

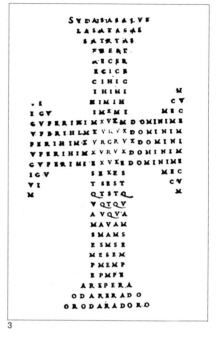

4,5,6. *Figurative compositions by El Lissitzky (1928).*
7. *A composition by I. C. Hittensperger (17th century). The calligraphic script takes the shape of a maze.*
11. *A calligram in Italian using text by Gabriel Garcia Marquez from 'One hundred years of solitude': 'Un filo di sangue uscì da sotto la porta, attraversò la sala, uscì in strada, continuò in un percorso diretto lungo i marciapiedi diseguali…'*
12. *A poetic text in Italian by Frederico Garcia Lorca: 'Ci sono anime che hanno / stelle azzurre, / mattini sfioriti / tra foglie del tempo…'*
13. *Laughing.*

8. *'Poème à Lou' by Guillaime Apollinaire taken from the story 'Poème à Lou' (1915).*
9. *Calligram by S. Nikuni titled 'Kawa Sasu' (sea beach).*
10. *'Forsythia' by M. E. Solt taken from the story 'Flowers in concrete' (1966).*

thanks to the use of calligraphic scripts (cf. fig. 7); some of the symbolic figures recurrent in this period are the 'hourglass', 'maze' and 'bottle'. Visual poetry for a long period becomes a very popular artistic genre: in Germany in particular there is a great profusion of humourous and amorous calligrams.

Subsequently, the spread of printing does not discourage the use of figurative texts which in many cases appear with ornamental characters; in different periods Laurence Sterne (1760) and Lewis Carroll (1860) break the texture of their texts with visual elaborations.

In the 20th century, the greatest representatives of the avant-garde search, using experimental letter combinations, new forms of poetic and artistic expression.

In Italy the Futurists theorise with their 'Tavole parolibere' (1912-1944) the breakage of the old typographic schemes; an extreme liberty in the order of words and letters has to favour the expression of states of mind and of the most profound sensations.

Cubists and Dadaists venture in the same years the particular use of typographic characters which are inserted in the most disparate works of art with an aesthetic finality but without loading them with linguistic and poetic valences.

Also within the sphere of the Bauhaus school, Moholy-Nagy gives rise to a new tendency in the 'communication of emotive forms' which however excludes the superimposition of text and image that is typical of the calligram.

The Russian Constructivists are the only ones to utilise visual composition by again exploiting the traditional link between the figurative and written parts; their graphic and typographic works have in fact an educational value, being considered instruments of struggle in a revolutionary programme (cf. figs. 4, 5 and 6).

More recently, thanks to the introduction of modern printing techniques, the game with typographic elements is open to numerous possibilities; there are many works carried out by the artists and graphics professionals that have engaged in this kind of expressive communication (cf. figs. 9 and 10).

11

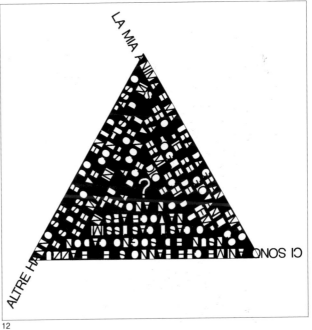

12

13

14

15

14. 'The fifth of May' by Alessandro Manzoni.
15. A composition based on a fingerprint.

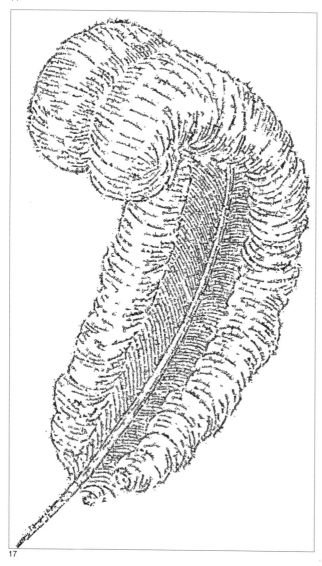

17

16

16. A composition based on the stars.
17. 'The graphic designer creates images' by Jean-Paul Sartre.

18

18. *A composition based on a portrait of Leonardo da Vinci;*
    the text is written from right to left.
19. *A Peruvian text based on a figure of the gigantic*
    drawings found in the Nazca desert in Peru.

19

Decorative alphabets

Designers of letters, graphic designers and even artists have engaged in the composition of new forms and particular decorations to be applied to letters. The idea for an alphabet different from the normal is born from the need for a communication which is more resistant to immediate decipherment and which is thus more interesting. These alphabets use letters so unusual that they cannot be used as ordinary characters for use in texts; they are designed for special graphics applications and find in these specific contexts their raison d'être.

The themes and methods of approach for the design of a new alphabet can be various; the examples shown here only show some. These new alphabets, while having purely decorative charateristics, appear only as capital letters.

Pre-arranged geometric scheme

The design of new letters starts with a pre-arranged geometric grid. Fig. 1a shows a geometric grid based on the diamond; inside this grid the x-height, ascenders and descenders are laid out (cf. figs. 1b and 1c) so that the letter assumes a diamond-like form, as one can see better from the overall image (cf. fig. 2).

In fig. 4 a second alphabet can be seen which is based on the shape of the diamond. The use of a grid which is less complex than the preceeding example reduces the opportunity to articulate the forms of the letters, which thus appear rigid and at times hard to read.

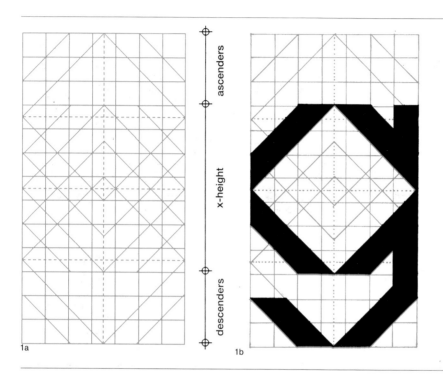
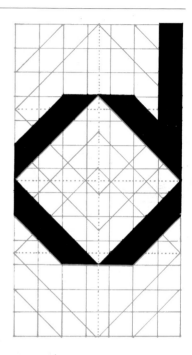

1a   1b   1c

ascenders

x-height

descenders

abcdeffghi
jklmnopqr;
stuuwxyz!?
1234567890

2

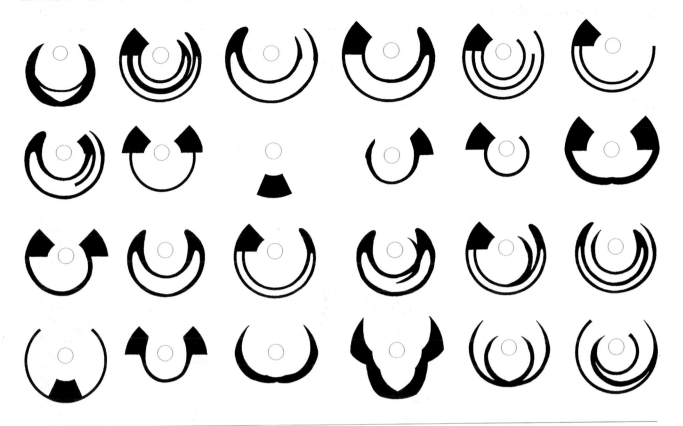

3a

The characters of fig. 3a are constructed according to an anamorphic geometric scheme; the letters are recomposed in their usual form only if projected onto the surface of a cylinder (cf. fig. 3b) of circumference equal to that indicated inside the drawing of each letter.

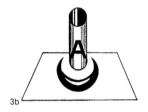

3b

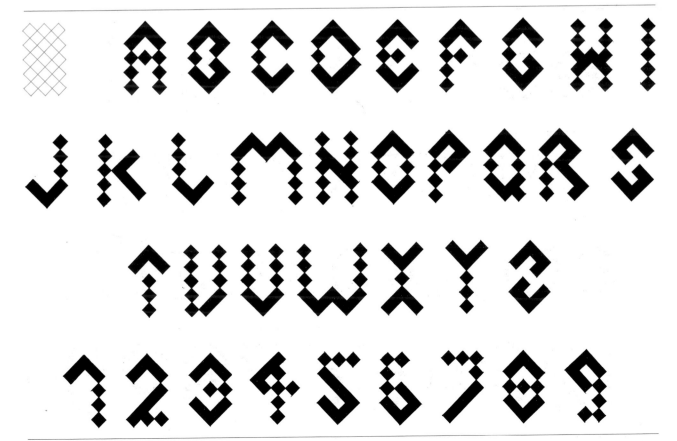

ABCDEFG
HILMNOP
QRSTUVZ

5

Objects of the same kind

By choosing objects of the same kind (flowers, plants, animals, tools, etc) one can create an arrangement of them which may give form to an alphabet.
The component objects may be adapted to the outline of a common typeface or otherwise be brought together in more original stylised forms.
In fig. 5 is shown an alphabet for illuminated signs where the letters take the shape of bent fluorescent tubes; in fig. 6 the classic shapes of an Old Style

typeface are read by means of the ordered flight of many bees; in fig. 7 the rigorous line of Helvetica are recomposed in a more fragmented manner by the pieces of a jigsaw puzzle; fig. 8 shows a curious alphabet composed with pieces of the track used for model car racing; finally the letters in fig. 9 are a version of that alphabet made from matches so often invented as a childrens' game.

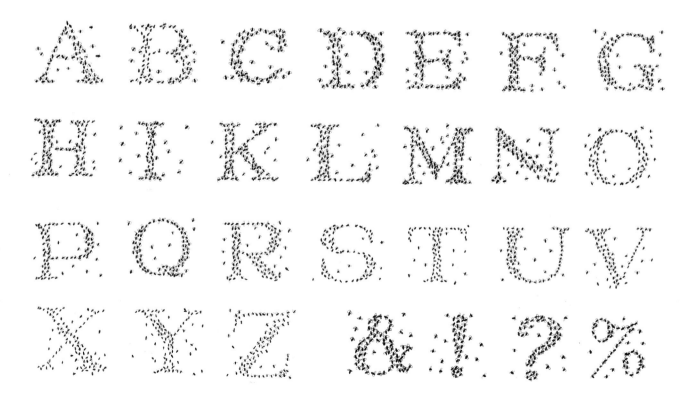

6

ABCDEFG
HILMNOP
QRSTUVZ

7

AUCCCEF GHI
JKLMNOPQ
RSTUVWXYZ

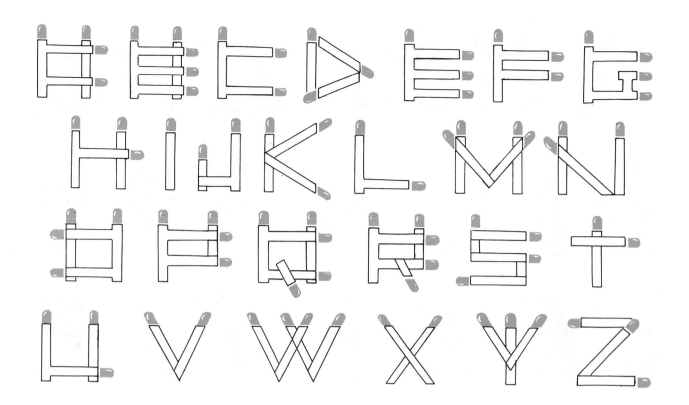

9

The sample letter

The creation of a new alphabet may start from the image of a single letter.
The constituent elements of this letter, beyond their decorative characteristics,
are the reference for the design of the whole alphabet.
In fig. 10 the shape of the letter 'A' has determinated the image of the others;
in some cases (letters H, K, T, X and Y) there is more than one possilble
version.

ABEFGH
HKKLPQR
TTXXYYW

10

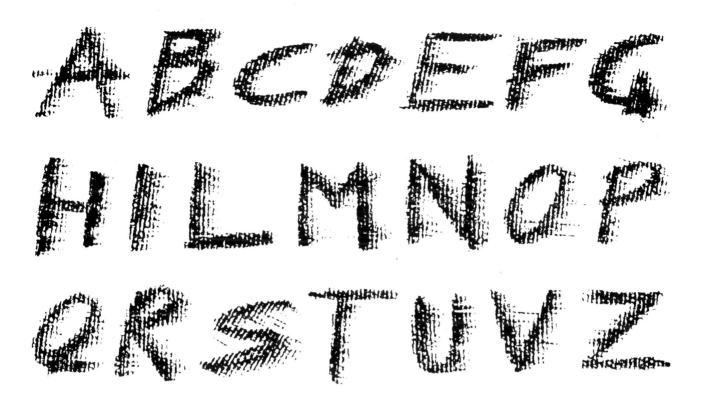

11

New techniques

Letters with singular forms at times can result from the simple application of
unusual writing techniques. The material with which one writes and the surface
adopted determined the originality of the overall image. The design realised
with charcoal on coarse-surfaced paper gives the alphabet of fig. 11 an
especially calligraphic aspect. In contrast, the letters of fig. 12 assume a
dynamic form thanks to the use of a cutting technique.

12

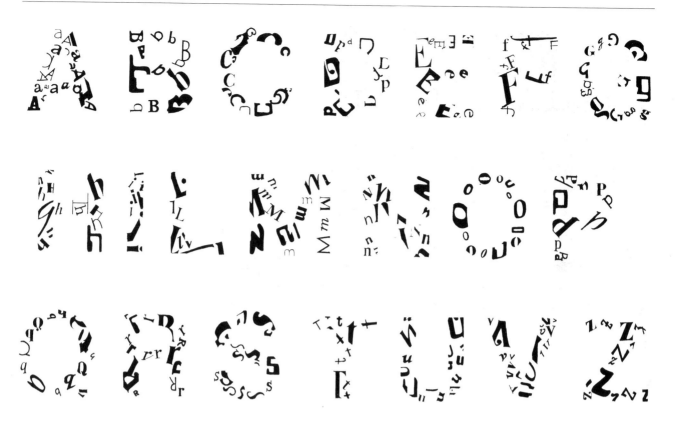

Textures

The customary image of a letter can take up different connotations simply by placing a texture on the surfaces of the stems that compose it.
In fig. 13 the strokes of the new alphabet are characterised by the design of a texture of…letters.

Pre-arranged style

The ways of figurative expression of artists differing styles can become the reference for the research into formal characteristics, linked to a precise style, on which to model the design of the letters; the characters of fig. 14 could be said to be in 'Kandinsky's style'.

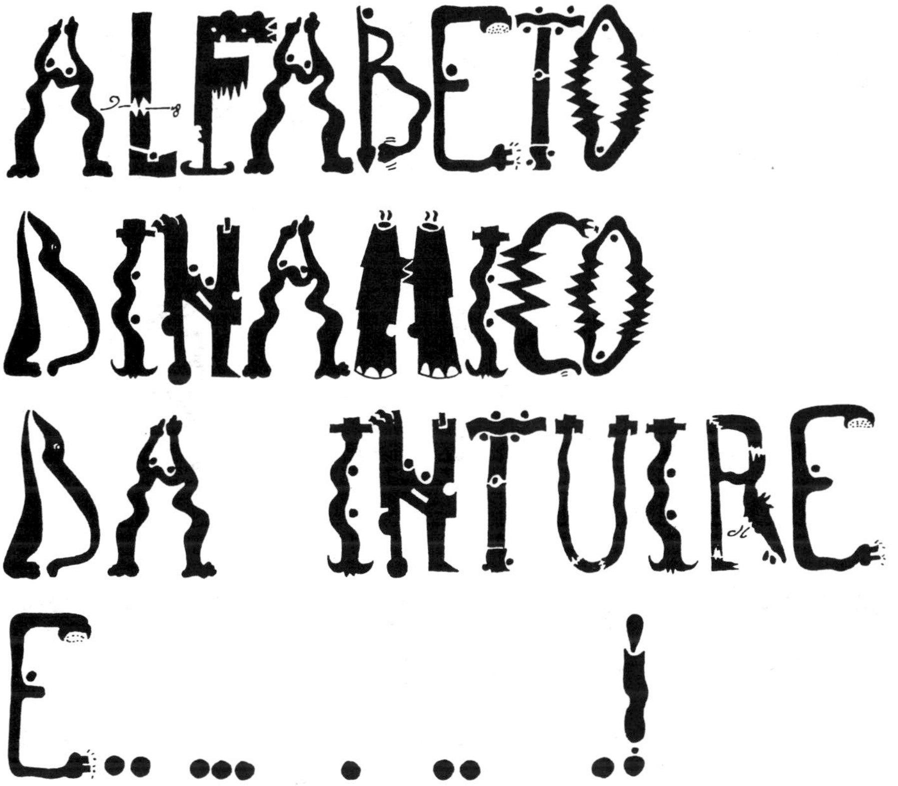

ALFABETO
DINAMICO
DA INTUIRE
E.... .. .!

15

The alphabet in fig. 15 and 16 does not fit in to any category described above; it is composed of figurative and decorative elements: it is in fact populated by characters, objects, curious animals and ornaments of eccentric shape. The result is however enthralling and of strong visual impact; the simple free play of creativity, uninhibited by references and conventions to pre-fixed characters, can give excellent results.

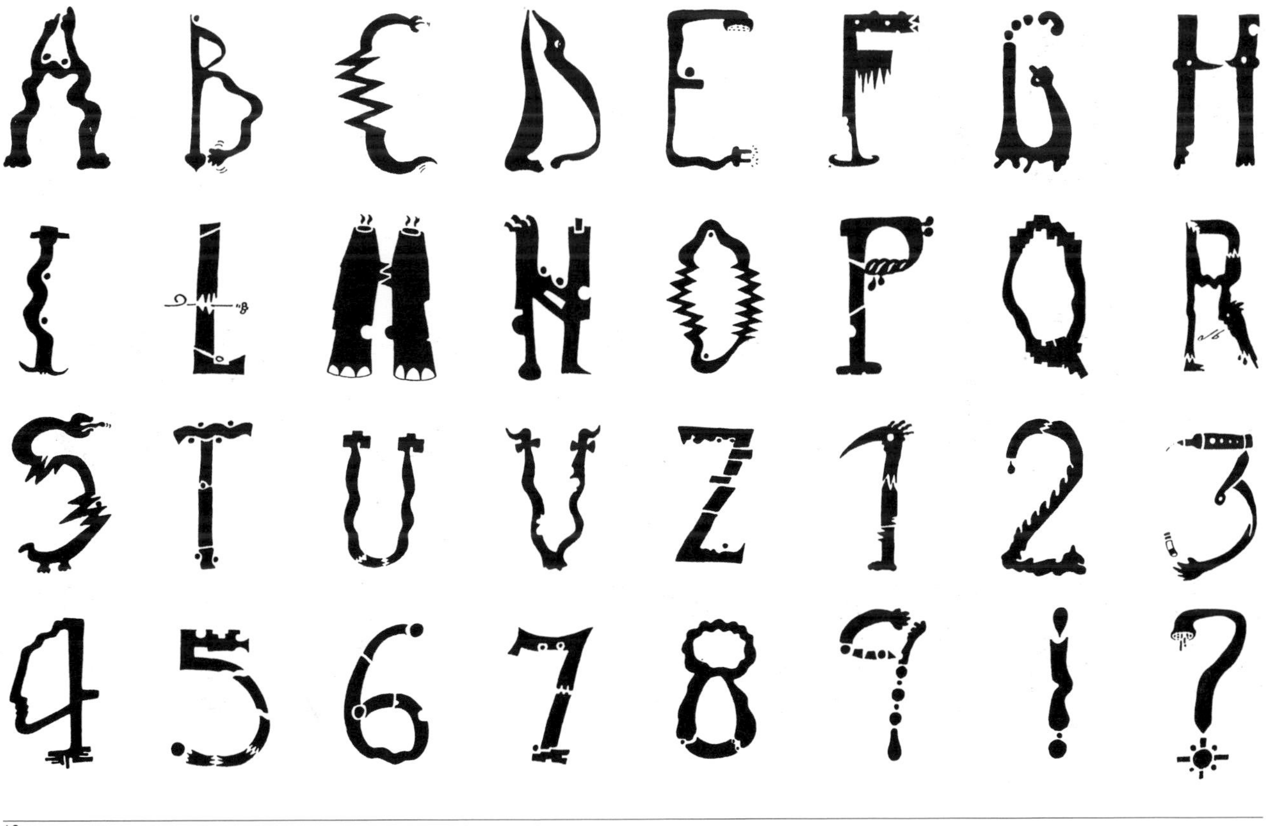

A B C D E F G H
I L M N O P Q R
S T U V Z 1 2 3
4 5 6 7 8 9 ! ?

16

The spread of alphabetic writing

The diagram on this page summarises the development of the principal modern alphabets from the original Phoenician. It is interesting to note how after its invention, this first phonetic alphabet undergoes many changes, becoming the Greek, Latin and Slavic alphabets while also being the basis for the many alphabets of India and the Middle East. Thanks to commercial and military expeditions, the Phoenician alphabet is spread to different cultural centres which adapt the its letters to the sounds of their own languages. Each civilisation invents new characters to suit its own needs and eliminates the superfluous letters, thus creating new alphabets.

The diagram on the opposite page shows in a more detailed form the evolution of the Latin alphabet by indicating the principal developments: from the first calligraphic scripts to the invention of printing with moveable type. Regarding the latter, the diagram describes its formal evolution using the names of the most important typefaces; the various branches represent the principal stylistic categories: Old Style, Modern, Egyptian, Sans Serif, Scripts, Display and Blackletter.

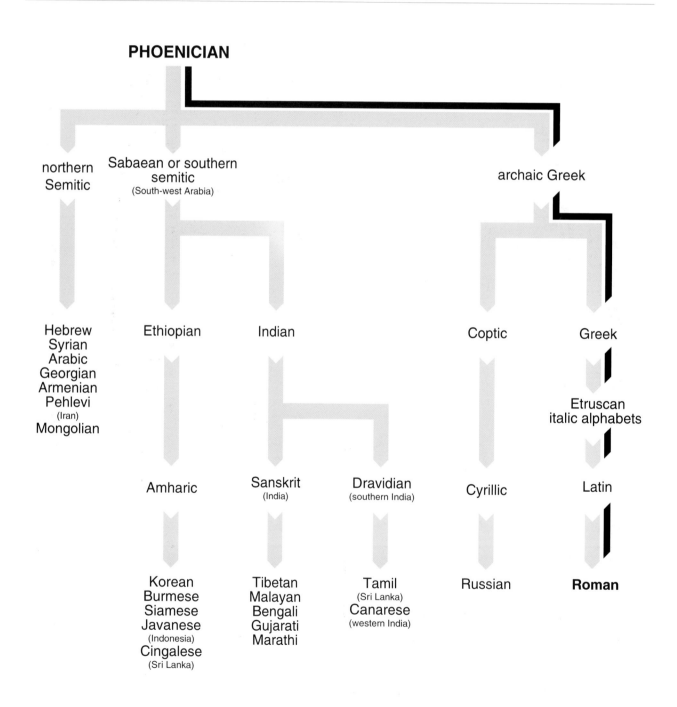

Stylistic evolution of Latin scripts and typefaces

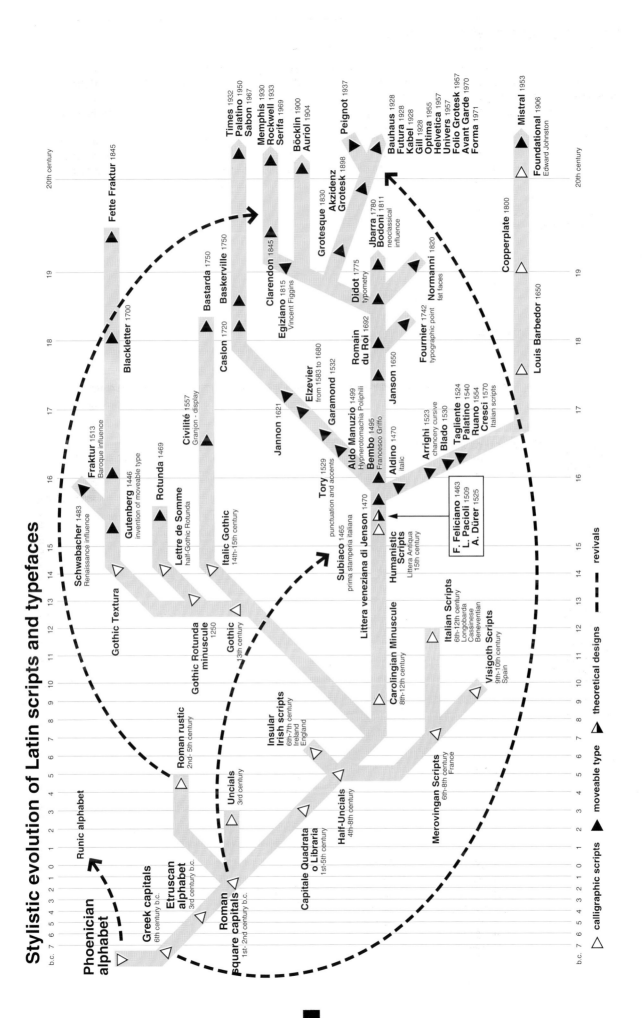

Phoenician alphabet

Runic alphabet

Greek capitals
6th century b.c.

Etruscan alphabet
3rd century b.c.

Roman rustic
2nd-5th century

Uncials
3rd century

Roman Square capitals
1st-2nd century b.c.

Capitale Quadrata o Libraria
1st-5th century

Half-Uncials
4th-8th century

Insular Irish scripts
6th-7th century
Ireland
England

Merovingan Scripts
6th-8th century
France

Carolingian Minuscule
8th-12th century

Italian Scripts
6th-12th century
Longobarda
Cassinese
Beneventian

Visigoth Scripts
9th-10th century
Spain

Schwabacher 1483
Renaissance influence

Gothic Textura

Gutenberg 1446
invention of moveable type

Gothic Rotunda minuscule
1250

Gothic
13th century

Fraktur 1513
Baroque influence

Rotunda 1469

Lettre de Somme
half-Gothic Rotunda

Italic Gothic
14th-15th century

Civilité 1557
Granjon - display

Fette Fraktur 1845

Blackletter 1700

Bastarda 1750

Baskerville 1750

Caslon 1720

Times 1932
Palatino 1950
Sabon 1967

Memphis 1930
Rockwell 1933
Serifa 1969

Böcklin 1900
Auriol 1904

Clarendon 1845

Egiziano 1815
Vincent Figgins

Grotesque 1830

Akzidenz Grotesk 1898

Peignot 1937

Bauhaus 1928
Futura 1928
Kabel 1928
Gill 1928
Optima 1955
Helvetica 1957
Univers 1957
Folio Grotesk 1957
Avant Garde 1970
Forma 1971

Jbarra 1780
Bodoni 1811
neoclassical influence

Didot 1775
typometry

Normanni 1820
fat faces

Romain du Roi 1692

Fournier 1742
typographic point

Louis Barbedor 1650

Copperplate 1800

Foundational 1906
Edward Johnston

Mistral 1953

Jannon 1621

Elzevier
from 1583 to 1680

Garamond 1532

Tory 1529
punctuation and accents

Subiaco 1465
prima stamperia italiana

Littera veneziana di Jenson 1470

Humanistic Scripts
Littera Antiqua
15th century

Aldo Manuzio 1499
Hypnerotomachia Poliphili

Bembo 1495
Francesco Griffo

Aldino 1470
italic

Arrighi 1523
chancery cursive

Blado 1530

Tagliente 1524
Palatino 1540
Ruano 1554
Cresci 1570
Italian scripts

Janson 1650

F. Feliciano 1463
L. Pacioli 1509
A. Dürer 1525

△ calligraphic scripts   ▲ moveable type   △ theoretical designs   - - - revivals

Glossary of technical terms

ascender
That part of a lower case letter which projects above the mean line.

bold
Typeface in which the stems are thicker than those of the regular version.

bustrofedic
An ancient writing system in which the lines of writing are made alternately from left to right and from right to left.

calligram
A poetic composition in which the words are laid out to create images related to the meaning of the text. The calligram is also known under the name of 'visual poetry'.

capital
Upper-case letter: the name comes from the Latin term 'Littera Capitalis'.

codex
In ancient Rome, wax tablets bound together to produce the first books. In the Middle Ages, books of three or four leaves of parchment folded once or twice.

colophon
In medieval manuscripts and the first printed books, a foot note giving the name of the work, the name of the author and the date and place of copying or printing. Today it is a brief wording, required by law, in which are stated the name of the printer, publisher and date of printing.

copperplate engraving
An engraving technique for the reproduction of images; incisions are made in copper plates (or other metals) either by a graver or by chemical means.

cuneiform
A script characterised by triangular marks created by the point of the special tool used to make them. The invention of cuneiform writing is attribuited to the Sumerians (3000 BC).

demotic
Writing of common use (from the Greek 'demotikòs' = popular) adopted in ancient Egypt; made with a brush on sheets of papyrus.

descender
That part of a lower case letter which projects below the base line.

digital
Represented by numbers; in contrast to analogue, to indicate operation in discrete states which work in steps and are not continous.

ductus
The movement made by the hand to draw a letter; of two kinds: writing and non-writing.

editio princeps
The first printed edition of a text previously known through manuscripts written before the invention of moveable type.

elzevier
A typeface belonging to the Old Style family. From the name Elzevier, the family of Dutch printers active between 1580 and 1712.

flourish
A special typographic character used for decorative purposes.

folio
Four pages achieved with a single fold of a sheet of paper.

grapheme
The smallest graphic unit in any writing system.

graver
A tool used for the engraving of wood and metal surfaces.

grotesque
A name given to some 19th century Sans Serif typeface.

hieratic
A script used in ancient Egypt by priests (from the Greek 'ieratikòs' = priestly); engraved in stone or written with a brush on papyrus.

incunabolo
A book printed between 1450 and c.1520, in the period in which first spread printing with moveable type.

italic
Born as a simulation of writing, any roman typeface with its letters inclined, usually to the right. Designed originally by Griffo for Manuzio as the Aldino typeface.

lapidary
A letter engraved in stone, the most famous of which are the Roman Square Capitals: the capital letters of the classical period.

lithography
A printing technique invented by Aloys Senefelder at the beginning of the 19th century. A flat-surface technique based on the principle of mutual repulsion between water and greasy substances. Initially a limestone slab was used and printing done with a hand press. Today this has been replaced by the offset litho machine which shares only the chemical process with the old technique; the stone having been replaced by metal sheets.

leading
A strip of metal alloy, of lesser height than that of type; used to space lines of text.

letterpress
Printing technique invented by Gutenberg in the first half of the 15th century. The printed elements (the moveable type) are in relief.

ligature
A character in which more than one letter is fused together to improve readability. the most common ligatures are made up of ff, fi, ffi,ffl.

logotype
A design in which the letters in the text find special links or particular forms which are more evocative of the subject.

matrix
Brass block which bears the impression of a letter made with a punch. One casts the type by pouring a quantity of metal into the cavity.

measure
The length of a line of text.

monogram
A graphic composition formed by two letters linked to each other in a particular manner.

old style
Definition used in Anglo-Saxon and generally in Nordic countries to distinguish roman and italic typefaces from Blackletter typefaces.

palimpsest
Parchment from which an old text has been erased in order to write a new one; with chemical processes today it is even possible to recover the original text.

parchment
A writing support made from skin of an animal, dried, treated and stretched-out to dry. In the form of the codex, it replaces the old papyrus rolls. With the invention of paper and printing it is used increasingly rarely and only for formal documents.

papyrus
A plant that grows principally in the Nile delta. The dried stalks, cut into strips and woven into a sheet are one of the earliest writing supports. The sheets are coiled in a roll (volumen) around a stick (umbilicum).

pica
Unit of typographic measurement equal to 12 points or approximately 1/6 inch.

pixel
Contraction of 'picture element'. The smallest base element of a digital image.

point
Typographic unit of measurement equal to 1/12 Pica.

punch
A block of hard steel which bears a letter at one end. With punches struck into the matrix, one produces the mould from the type is cast.

quads
Pieces of metal which being below the height of type create word spacing. They are generally in the following widths: em, 2, 3 and 4 ems.

quill-pen
Writing instrument. The ancients used pens from various birds but those of the goose were the most popular for their softness and flexibility.

recto
The right-hand page of an open book.

reed pen
A writing instrument made from a reed with a cut nib; used originally by the ancient Egyptians and until the 6th century AD.

roman
Upright letters, having no inclination.

sans serif
A typeface without serifs.

screwpress
A hand-operated machine contemporary with Gutenberg. It comprises a surface on which are placed the type and a second surface which is lowered mechanically onto the former to apply pressure.

scribe
A copier or creator of handwritten texts.

scriptorium	A room in a monastery in which medieval scribes went to carry out the work of copying and illuminating.		**type**	A small block in metal alloy on whose upper face is carried the image of a letter or mark. The same term is commonly used to mean the whole alphabet.
seal	A graphic composition of two or more letters linked together in a particular manner.		**typeface**	An alphabet, usually in upper and lower case letters and with numerals and punctuation. Individually characterised by a unified style common to all the characters that it contains.
serif	The projecting, finishing strokes at the ends of stems.		**umbilicum**	A stick around which are rolled sheets of papyrus.
shoulder	The perimeter of the type body not occupied by the letter.		**verso**	The left-hand page of an open book.
size	Defines the size of a typeface and is the height of the type body.		**volumen**	Ancient manuscript rolled around a stick known as an umbilicum.
small capitals	Capital letters of reduced height, equal to the typeface's x-height.		**woodcutting**	Engraving in wood; drawing are engraved back to front.
stem	The essential linear elements of a letter 'Plein' in French, 'Asta'in Italian, 'Abstrich' in German.		**x-height**	The height of the lower case letters, measured from the base line to the mean line.
stencil	Letters which, made with the use of a perforated plate, have separated stems.			

Directory of the principal typefaces for editorial use

Here are indicated the name of the typeface, the foundry which holds the matrices, the year of publication and the name of the designer. (Where the name of the designer is not indicated, the typeface was designed wholly by the foundry.)

SANS SERIF

Akzidenz Grotesk	Berthold 1898
Antique Olive	Marcel Olive 1962 - R. Excoffon
Avant-Garde	ITC 1970 - H. Lubalin, T. Carnase
Eurostile	Nebiolo 1962 - A. Novarese
Folio	Bauer 1957/62 - K. F. Bauer, W. Baum
Frutiger	Linotype 1976 - A. Frutiger
Futura	Bauer 1927/30 - P. Renner
Gill Sans	Monotype 1928/30 - E. Gill
Helvetica	Haas 1957 - M. Miedinger
Kabel	Klingspor Type Foundry 1927 - R. Koch
Optima	Stempel 1958 - H. Zapf
Univers	Deberny 1957 - A.Frutiger

EGYPTIAN

Beton	Fundación Tipografica Neutville 1936 - H. Jost
City	Berthold 1930 - G. Trump
Clarendon	Haas 1951/53 - H.Eidenbenzen
Egizio	Nebiolo 1955/58 - A. Novarese
Melior	Stempel 1952 - H. Zapf
Memphis	Stempel 1929 - R. Wolf
Rockwell	Monotype 1934
Serifa	Bauersche Griesserei 1969 - A. Frutiger

OLD STYLE

Blado	Monotype 1923 - from Arrighi's italic scripts
Bembo	Monotype 1929 - from F. Griffo
Baskerville	ATF 1959 - T. Thompson from J. Baskerville
Caslon	ATF 1960 - from W. Caslon
Centaur	Monotype 1914/29 - B. Rogers from N. Jenson
Century	ATF 1900 - M. F. Benton,
Garamond	ATF 1917 - M. F. Benton, T. M. Cleland from C. Garamond
Goudy Old Style	ATF 1915/28 - F. W. Goudy
Imprimatur	Bauer 1952 - K. F. Bauer, W. Baum
Meridien	Deberny 1955 - A. Frutiger
Paganini	Nebiolo 1928 - A. Butti, R. Bertieri
Palatino	Stempel 1948/51 - H. Zapf
Perpetua	Monotype 1927 - E. Gill
Plantin	Monotype 1929 - F. H. Pierport from Plantin
Sabon	Stempel 1965 - J. Tschichold
Times New Roman	Monotype 1931 - S. Morison (327 is the original version)
Van Dijck	Monotype 1935 - J. van Krimpen from C. V. Dijck

MODERN

Bodoni	Bauer 1926 - from G. B. Bodoni
Walbaum	Berthold 1976 - G.G. Lange da J.E. Walbaum
Zapf book	ITC 1967 - H. Zapf

Bibliography

Various	Bodoni. L'invenzione della semplicità. Ugo Guanda Editore, Parma. 1990
V. Accame	Il segno poetico. Edizioni d'arte Zarathustra, Milan. 1981
M. Andersch	Tracce, segni, caratteri. Ulisse Edizioni, Turin. 1989
A. Bandinelli **G. Lussu** **R. Iacobelli**	Farsi un libro. Biblioteca del Vascello / Stampa alternativa, Rome. 1990
R. Barthes	L'ovvio e l'ottuso. Einaudi, Turin. 1985
A. Bartram	Lettering in Architecture. Lund Humphries, London. 1975
B. Binns	Better type. Watson Guptill Publications, New York. 1989
L. Blackwell	Twentieth-Century type. Laurence King Publishing, London. 1992
E. M. Catich	The origin of the serif. Catich Gallery. St. Ambrose University, Davenport. 1991
D. Diringer	L'alfabeto nella storia della civiltà. Giunti B. Barbera, Florence. 1969
M. Drogin	Medieval calligraphy. Its history and technique. Prior, London. 1980
R. Druet **H. Gregoire**	La civilisation de l'écriture. Fayard et Dessain et Toira, Paris. 1976
S. Fabris **R. Germani**	Disegno di lettere. Società Editrice Internazionale, Turin. 1967
E. Fazzioli	Caratteri cinesi. Arnoldo Mondadori Editore, Milan. 1986
F. Feliciano Veronese	Alphabetum Romanum by G. Mardersteig. Editiones Officinae Bodoni, Verona. 1960
G Fioravanti	Grafica e stampa. Zanichelli, Bologna. 1984
K. Földess-Papp	Dai graffiti all'alfabeto. Jaca Book, Milan. 1985
A. Frutiger	Des signes et des hommes. Editions Delta & Spes, Lausanne. 1983
L. Fumanelli	Il carattere nella storia e nell'arte della stampa. Centro arte e mestieri, Fondazione G. Cini, Venice. 1965
N. Gray	A history of lettering. Phaidon Press, London. 1986
S. Gregorietti **E. Vassalle**	La forma della scrittura. Tipologia e storia degli alfabeti dai Sumeri ai giorni nostri. Feltrinelli, Milan. 1988
A. Haab **A. Stocker**	Lettera. A. Niggli + W. Verkau, Teufen-St.Gallen. 1954
M. Harvey	Creative lettering. The Bodley Head, London. 1985
	Calligraphy in the graphic art. The Bodley Head, London. 1988
A. Hohenegger	Forma e segno dell'alfabeto e del simbolo. Romana libri Alfabeto, Rome. 1977
	Graphic design. Romana libri Alfabeto, Rome. 1974
J. Hutchinson	Letters. The Herbert Press, London. 1983
G. Iliprandi	Linguaggio grafico. 3 vols., Editoriale A-Z, Milan. 1983
D. Jackson	The story of writing. Studio Vista, London - Cassel. 1981
G. Jean	L'écriture mémoire des hommes. Découvertes Gallimard, Paris. 1987
E. Johnston	Writing & Illuminating, and Lettering. Black, USA. 1987
R. Koch	The book of signs. First Edition Club, London. 1930
Y. Kuwaya	Trade marks and symbols: alphabetical designs. Van Nostrand Reinhold Company, New York. 1973
S. Morison	First principles of typography. Inside: Books and Printing. The Monotype Corporation Ltd., Cleveland-N.Y. 1963
E. Nerdinger	Zeichen Schrift + Ornament. Verlag G. Callwey, Munchen. 1960
B. Neuenschwander	Letterwork. Creative letterforms in Graphic Design Phaidon Press Ltd, London. 1993.
A. Novarese	Alfa-beta. Lo studio e il disegno del carattere. Progresso grafico, Turin. 1964
	Il segno alfabetico. Progresso Grafico, Turin. 1971
J. Peignot	De l'écriture à la typographie. Gallimard, Paris. 1967
	Du calligram. Dossiers graphiques du Chêne, Paris. 1978
	Du chiffre. Jacques Damase Editeur, Paris. 1982
G. Pellitteri **G. Stefanelli**	Il carattere. Edizioni Raggio, Rome. 1947
A. Petrucci	La scrittura. Piccola Biblioteca Einaudi, Turin. 1980
	Medioevo da leggere. Piccola Biblioteca Einaudi, Turin. 1992
R. Queneau	Segni, cifre e lettere. Einaudi letteratura, Turin. 1981
E. Ruder	Typographie. A manual of design. Verlag Arthur Niggli, Heiden AR. 1988
M. Stribley	The calligraphy source book. Quarto Publishing Ltd, London. 1986
H. Spencer	The liberated page. Lund Humphries, London. 1987
S. H. Steinberg	Cinque secoli di stampa. Piccola Biblioteca Einaudi, Turin. 1962
D. B. Updike	Some tendencies in modern typography. Inside: Books and Printing. The Monotype Corporation Ltd., Cleveland-N.Y. 1963
C. Weigel	Della scrittura quadrata. Dante Bertieri, Milan. 1962
H. M. Wingler	The Bauhaus Weimar, Dessau, Berlin, Chicago. The MIT Press Cambridge, Massachusetts. 1969
J. Woodcock	A book of formal scripts. A&C Black, London. 1992
H. Zapf	Manuale Typographicum Z-Presse, Frankfurt. 1968
	Dalla calligrafia alla composizione. Edizioni Valdonega, Verona. 1991